Biblical Confessions for Financial Prosperity

Proverbs 18:21 says that death and life are in the power of the tongue, therefore, I speak the Word of God concerning my finances:

1. **The favor of God surrounds me and precedes me.**

    Psalm 5:12, Proverbs 11:27, Proverbs 12:2

2. **The blessings of God are chasing me and overtaking me.**

    Deuteronomy 28:1-2, Luke 6:38

3. **Whatever I set my hand to shall prosper.**

    Joshua 1:8, Psalm 1:3, Psalm 35:27, III John 2

4. **My Heavenly Father gives me power to get wealth.**

    Deuteronomy 8:18, Proverbs 8:17-21, II Corinthians 8:9

5. **God is liberally supplying all my needs according to His riches in glory by Christ Jesus.**

    Philippians 4:19, Proverbs 3:9-10, Matthew 6:8 & 33

6. **I no longer live under the curse of poverty. The windows of Heaven are open to me, and God rebukes the devourer for my sake.**

    Malachi 3:8-12, Galatians 3:13-14

7. **The Lord has commanded me to be blessed, therefore, I am blessed and cannot be cursed. I am the head and not the tail. I am above only and not beneath. I will lend and not borrow.**

    Deuteronomy 28:3-14, Proverbs 10:6

If Charles And Frances Can Do It,
YOU Can Do It, Too!

by

Charles and Frances Hunter

Books by Charles ✝ Frances Hunter

A Confession A Day Keeps The Devil Away
Angels On Assignment
Are You Tired?
Born Again! What Do You Mean?
Come Alive
Follow Me
Go, Man, Go!
God Is Fabulous
God's Answer To Fat...LOØSE IT!
Handbook For Healing
Hang Loose With Jesus
Heart To Heart Flip Chart
His Power Through You
Holy Laughter
Hot Line To Heaven
How Do You Treat My Son Jesus?
How To Heal The Sick
How To Make Your Marriage Exciting
How To Pick A Perfect Husband...Or Wife
How To Receive & Maintain A Healing
How To Receive & Minister The Baptism With The Holy Spirit
I Don't Follow Signs & Wonders...They Follow Me
If You Reallly Love Me...
Impossible Miracles
Let This Mind Be In You
Memorizing Made Easy
P.T.L.A. (Praise The Lord Anyway)
the fabulous Skinnie Minnie Recipe Book
Strength For Today
Supernatural Horizons (From Glory To Glory)
The Two Sides Of A Coin
Video Study Guide-How To Heal The Sick (15 Hours)
Video Study Guide-How To Heal The Sick Power Pack (6 Hours)
What Is Real Prosperity?
Why Should "I" Speak In Tongues?
You Can Do It, Too

Scripture quotations are taken from:
The New King James Version (NKJV), used throughout unless otherwise noted.
©1983 by Thomas Nelson, Inc., Nashville, Tennessee
The Authorized King James Version (KJV)
The Living Bible, Paraphrased (TLB)
©1971 by Tyndale House Publishers, Wheaton, Illinois
The Amplified Old Testament (Amp)
©1965 by Zondervan Publishing
The Amplified New Testament (Amp)
©1954, 1958, The Lockman Foundation

Table Of Contents

If Charles And Frances Can Do It,
YOU Can Do It, Too!

Chapter One

If Charles And Frances Can Do It,
YOU Can Do It, Too!

The most awesome, thrilling, exciting, and humbling experience in the world is to lay hands on someone and see them recover instantly before your eyes! This should be an everyday experience for all Christian believers because Jesus said the believers would lay hands on the sick and they would recover. He even went so far as to say in John 14:12 that the believers would not only do the same things He did but they would do greater works than these "because I go to My Father!" What a glorious time to be a part of the fulfillment of this scripture.

Prior to returning to heaven, Jesus said *"All authority has been given to Me in heaven and on earth"* (Matt. 28:18). In Luke 10:19 He said, *"Behold, I give you the authority to trample on serpents and scorpions, and over all the power of the enemy, and nothing shall by any means hurt you!"* Why did He do that? Because He was returning to heaven so that He could be supernaturally reproduced in those who would believe.

One of the most thrilling things in our ministry is to see how the believers are latching on to the idea that God actually does want all of us to lay hands on the sick and that Jesus sent back the Holy Spirit so we would all have the same power and authority that He had to heal the sick.

5

You and I are living in the most exciting days in which a Christian has ever had the opportunity to be alive. You and I are seeing demonstrations of the Holy Spirit which have not been seen even in the days of the disciples.

Recently we were ministering on "The Holy Ghost and Fire" when suddenly the pastor stood up and said, "I'm about to freak out!" I was so shocked when he said this because I wondered what I had said that caused his reaction. But he continued, "I hear the wind of the Spirit blowing! It's so awesome, I'm scared!" 750 of the people who were at that meeting instantly stood up and screamed, "I hear the wind, too!"

There was a woman who had a word from the Lord but she wrote it on a piece of paper after this happened. I didn't receive it until the next night but this is what it said:

"Last night you heard the stirring of a mighty rushing wind,
But that is not the ending, it's just where I begin.
Tonight expect the currents that will lift you to the heights,
But it won't be done by power, it won't be done by might.
I'll lift you by My Spirit to a place you've yet to see,
I'll raise you to a level that unveils the mystery.
You'll view an inner kingdom where the supernatural reigns,
And I'll reveal the blueprints to build a new domain.
I'll sweep you up to glory and let you view My plans,
But you must stand believing and trusting that I can.
Tonight's the night I promised to many yielded hearts,

So from your flesh get ready to humbly depart.
Be fervent in your praises and come to higher realms,
For all you've hoped and prayed for is up here where
I am."

We believe that word is for every person who reads this book. We all want to go up on a higher level where the Holy Ghost is concerned. God wants us to believe that He is who He is and that He can do anything and that absolutely nothing is impossible with God. We all say it with our mouths. We all say it with our heads, "Nothing is impossible with God." But we need to get it way down deep into our hearts. When we say, "Nothing is impossible with God," we need to believe it with all of our mind, our heart, our body and soul.

Head knowledge is no good. Lip service is no good. This belief has to be implanted so deep in your heart that you won't ever limit God. We're so foolish when we limit God because if God created the universe – He can do anything. He can do anything and everything! And He will do it for you!

Grace – Airline Booking Agent

Grace has been with the airlines six years, spending every day meeting people, most of them on the phone; talking about their plans to travel to all sorts of places, and helping them with many of the questions for which they really need answers. It's a job that really warms her heart because it makes her feel useful and needed.

In the short breaks between calls she has time to reflect on the events in her life during the last year or so.

It's been several years now since she committed her life to Jesus Christ. What a change that made! It seemed to give everything else real meaning.

As a single parent, Grace and her daughter, Maureen, have grown closer and closer through the relationship they both have with the Lord.

Exciting things began to happen when she enrolled in the Hunter Healing School. The announcement had mentioned that we would be coming to San Antonio in December to hold a giant Healing Explosion. That sounded great, but the awesome thing was that the Healing School students were told that during the meeting, the people who would be praying for the sick would not be the Hunters, but just ordinary believers who were trained through the "How To Heal The Sick" video course. Grace wondered if it was possible that she could be one of those people?

It certainly seemed worth looking into.

Grace thought the first session of the video school was good, hearing about the vision we reported that confirmed what God had spoken to us several years previously. The Body of Christ had been seen rising up and standing tall on the earth. Demons were seen scattering from this new wave of power and authority. And the ones doing all this were the everyday, ordinary believers – just like Grace and thousands of others going forth and laying hands on the sick.

It was after several sessions that Grace really began to see the impact of what was being said. The effect was so great on her that she became unsure of her salvation.

She had never before laid hands on anyone and seen them healed!

She had never cast out even one demon! Yet there it was! Right in God's Word! *"These signs will follow those who believe: In My name they will cast out devils... they will lay hands on the sick and they will recover."*

She questioned if she was even a believer! Slowly she began to realize that, yes, she was born again, but she had never been told that she was supposed to be out doing these things.

If she had only known! How could she be doing these things if she had never been told? But now *she* had been told! And never again would she be satisfied with anything less. If this is what Jesus had commanded her to do, then by His grace that is exactly what she would do. It did not seem possible that God could use her that way, but if He would, then He most certainly could! So she made herself available to the Holy Spirit to be used in just whatever way He desired.

Her first opportunity had come just a short while after that commitment.

The day had been routine; a day like so many others. Grace had been pretty busy that morning, taking calls from people wanting to go just about every place Southwest Airlines went, and some places she had never even heard of. Soon a break was well in order. A cool refreshing drink and a few minutes to relax would surely help.

She went into the ladies' lounge and at first she didn't notice a lady co-worker standing at the sink. She was leaning on the sink, one hand on either side of it, holding on. Suddenly Grace was prompted by the Holy Spirit to approach her. She asked the woman what the problem was. In obvious pain, she told Grace that she was having tremendous pain in her kidneys. She'd had some kidney problems and now the pain was really getting to her.

Quickly Grace "checked" in the Spirit. It was sort

of a "am I on the right track" check. Knowing that she was, she proceeded. She told the woman that she was going to place her hands on her back in the area of her kidneys, and ask Jesus to heal her. Then she commanded that all the pain leave in the name of Jesus, and that all the parts connected with the kidneys be healed.

Grace then picked up her purse and walked out of the ladies' room.

She did not see the woman for three days. The reason was simple! Grace took a three day break and just relaxed.

When she returned, she was met by a very excited woman. The lady from the "ladies' lounge encounter" exclaimed that within 15 minutes all the pain was gone and that there had been no further problem!

Word of this miraculous event spread, and others began coming to Grace for healing. She began to see that when people experienced the real power of God, not just religion, they talk about it, they tell others. In turn, many of those who hear want that same touch.

Yolanda was that way. Her little son had developed a very high fever and a lump on the side of his neck. Her first thought had been to get him to a doctor – quickly. The doctor had told her that unless the fever and the infection were both gone by later in the day he would have to put the child into the hospital. As Yolanda left the doctor's office, she remembered the stories being told about the lady at work who was supposed to be able to heal sick people in the name of Jesus. What if it were all true? It surely would beat a stay in the hospital! It surely would be worth a try.

She got to the office just as Grace was arriving at

work. She explained the problem and Grace responded by placing her hand on the lump and simply commanding the fever and the infection to leave "In Jesus' name."

A miracle happened! The fever broke at once! Shortly afterwards the lump was gone.

Grace has been used many times since then, both at work and at church, to minister healing.

One of the most interesting and exciting things happened as she, her daughter and her mother sat down to enjoy a good meal in a local restaurant.

As Grace was ordering her meal, suddenly that gentle nudging of the Holy Spirit for which she had learned to listen became evident.

Her attention was called to a group of people sitting at a nearby table. The restaurant was crowded since it was during the noon rush, but the Lord singled out just the people at that one table. Grace was then divinely impressed with a word of knowledge that one of the people at that particular table was experiencing pain as a result of a bad back problem.

She knew God wanted to heal that person immediately, right in the restaurant.

With a sense of awe and trembling, Grace approached the table. She introduced herself to the people and explained why she was there. At first she received some looks of shock and almost disbelief, but then they all pointed to one gentleman seated with them.

This man had been injured at work and had back trouble! His back was hurting at that very moment so he was quick to respond. He wanted to be rid of the pain!

He asked Grace what she wanted him to do and she had him stand up right there in that crowded restaurant.

Fear and apprehension gone now, faith was rising. She did the "total" thing on him and he was instantly healed. The pain left!

She instructed him to try to do what he could not do before. He bent over and touched the floor – he had been touched by the power of God! Nobody objected. Nobody said a word. But they did watch, and they did see!

We must keep uppermost in our minds the purpose of healing. Jesus did miracles so people would believe in Him and be saved. It is always a great thrill when people accept Jesus and we have the pleasure of taking them to church and seeing them mature in Him!

Grace knows now that no matter how long she may stay on this earth, she has found what the Holy Spirit wants her to spend her life doing. She has come to know something else; something that she can tell all her saved friends! If you have been born again and received the baptism with the Holy Spirit, what Grace is doing is also what Jesus wants you to do too!

Al – A Christian Cop

It was during the time of year when most folks in the United States have what they call winter. They call it winter in San Antonio too, but it's certainly not like what takes place up north. In Texas a winter day may get down to 45 degrees and we consider that a cold day. It was that kind of day when Al, a police officer, was patrolling one of the many parks in San Antonio.

Not much was taking place: a few persistent joggers were there, wearing their long sweats, and a few even wearing ski masks. For the most part, it was a really quiet day.

As Al drove around in the patrol car, winding through the narrow streets that carried picnickers and general park-goers to the various tabled areas, he allowed his mind to carry him back to those events which marked what was to be the beginning of the most exciting time of his life.

Al's wife, Linda had enthusiastically attended the first meeting of the "How To Heal The Sick" video class at their church. He didn't know a whole lot about us or what we did. He had only been saved about two years and he knew there were a lot of things going on he didn't understand. Al didn't attend the class, though, since he had to work on the night the class was being held.

He remembered those times when he got home from patrolling his shift and Linda would have been to the Healing School. She would be almost ecstatic about what she had heard and seen: "growing out legs and arms" and all sorts of things that sounded pretty far out to Al.

Suddenly, as Al was driving around the park think-ing over these things, his mind was yanked back to the present as he heard a commotion in some trees and un-derbrush. He pulled to the edge of the grass and shut off the engine. At that moment, four kids came running out of the brush and almost crashed headlong into the side of the car. Their eyes went wide when they had to pull up short, almost eyeball to eyeball with the light flasher bar on top of Al's patrol car. He told them to be careful and stay out of the brush and on the paths that zig-zag all through the park. They trotted off, sheepishly laughing and waving back at him. Al then resumed his casual pa-trol of the area and his mind resumed its recounting hap-penings of the previous few months.

Linda had told Al just about everything she had

learned during the video class. For fifteen hours she had watched us give instructions on healing. There had been plenty of testimonies to verify that "if Charles and Frances can do it, YOU can do it, too!" This concept had stirred something deep down inside Al and he thought it was awesome to think that he could lay his hands on a sick person and see God's power heal them.

Linda had told him how she had been taught that healing the sick was not just a matter of praying, but it involved speaking to the illness in the name of Jesus Christ and commanding healing to come. Al had never heard that before.

He pulled out onto one of the main streets that bordered the park and headed for the closest convenience store for a quick cup of coffee. Once again Al began to recall certain life-changing events that had occurred recently. His mind zeroed in on the one event which so impacted his entire life that he could recall each detail as though it had happened only minutes ago.

The sun had already set over San Antonio and Al was on patrol at Woodlawn Lake. With the setting of the sun, the gentle breeze which had been brushing the lake into little ripples had died away. Now the only noise was the sound of the stubborn picnickers who just refused to allow the day to draw to a close.

The lake was peacefully calm – and quickly disappearing to the eye as dusk passed and night was drawing its dark curtain over the trees on the far bank. Slowly it moved over the lake until it began to black out even the brush and trees close to the gate where Al and his partner had parked their patrol car. As they sat there, each deep in his own thoughts, they were suddenly jolted back to reality by the frantic sounds of someone telling them that a man had fallen into the lake and drowned!

The two patrolmen were quickly informed that the man had been seen going under the water some 15-20 minutes before. The witness pointed to the general area where the victim was last seen.

Racing to the spot, Al tried to peer through the darkness to catch a glimpse of something – anything that might look like someone in the water – but he could see nothing! It was just too dark! He turned on his flashlight and shined it over the top of the water.

Everything was deathly still! There was no movement to indicate the man was still above the water. Nothing! Only silence.

Suddenly someone standing next to Al shouted that he saw something.

"Where?" Al shouted!

"There!" was the reply.

Al pointed the light where the man had indicated. His heart sank! He saw nothing!

The man then took the flashlight from Al and splashed a beam of light to the spot where he was sure he had caught just a glimmer of something. Something was there under the water, just beneath the dark surface.

Al quickly discarded his gun belt and dove into the water. Within a matter of seconds he had reached the spot where he was sure he had seen something. As he grabbed out toward that spot, his hand closed on a shirt. Beneath the shirt he could feel only cold flesh.

Frantically, Al pulled upward to try to get the man's head out of the water. The water was not very deep, so he stood up and tried to locate any sign of life. Nothing!

The man seemed to be cold and getting stiff.

Quickly Al's mind began to calculate. According to the witness the man had been under the water for twenty minutes by now and maybe more! Al thought, "He couldn't be alive! Human beings just don't survive that long under water!"

Al began to pray silently, "He is dead! No, Lord! My heart cries out for his life! Please Lord, let him be alive!"

He reached the shore and his partner helped pull both of them out of the water. Again they checked for any sign of life – and found nothing.

Al thought the man could possibly be breathing and looked for some sign, any kind of sign! None. The man is dead! Al's heart cried out, "NO!"

At that point, Al's partner began CPR. The victim did not respond and Al's partner began to tire.

Now it was Al's turn! "Lord, let him live!"

Desperately Al pounded on the man's chest trying to get his heart to beat. Nothing! He went through all the steps of CPR as he had been taught. Still, nothing! Then, from the depth of Al's being and up into his mind came a thought. Right from the Spirit of God Al recalled something his wife had told him that we had said about this kind of situation. It was something about commanding life to enter – about "binding the power of death." He remembered that we had even said to command the water to leave the lungs.

Al wondered, "Could it be? This man is dead! Could it work?"

There was no time to debate and no time to doubt!

Al stood with a boldness not of himself and commanded the spirit of death to go in the name of Jesus. He commanded life to re-enter this man. Boldness came into Al's heart with his rising faith! Once again he commanded life to return and the man's lungs to empty.

Suddenly, the man sat up and started coughing mud out of his lungs!

With its siren screaming, the ambulance arrived and the attendants jumped out. "Where's the dead man?" they shouted.

"Over here," was the reply.

They looked at the man who had come back to life and said, "No, we want the dead man."

Much to their surprise, the "dead man" was sitting there, breathing normally!

Al went to the hospital the next week and led the "dead man" to Jesus. His name was Moses!

Al says that this was the most exciting time of his life! He remembers the holy awe he felt some weeks later as Moses stood before the crowd at the church and testified as to how God had brought him back to life and given him another chance.

It wasn't long after that when Al received a call from the Chief's office. It was the voice of his boss, the police sergeant.

"Are you the one who allegedly raised a man from the dead out at Woodlawn Lake?" The shock struck Al with fear, realizing that this was not a normal event for a policeman. He thought, "Oh, oh, I'm in trouble!"

The sergeant continued, "I want to see you in my office right away!"

"Yes, sir!" Al answered.

A few minutes later Al stood in front of the sergeant

who asked him to tell the whole story. He did, all the time wondering what the sergeant's reaction would be.

His reply stunned Al for a moment as he said, "I'm a Spirit-filled Christian, too. Let's form a group of Spirit-filled policemen and train them to do what God wants us to do."

As a result, a new police organization was born. It is called "Shields for Christ" and they are having a monthly meeting and it is growing. They even have hopes of seeing this become a national organization! The want all the members to take the video healing school training so they can know how to direct God's Holy Spirit power for His glory. Hallelujah! As Al pulled into the parking lot at "Stop and Go" he gratefully thought, "How great is our God. What a neat Savior we have!"

The "Stop and Go" was almost deserted as Al walked back to the coffee pot. He had been there plenty of times before, so he spoke to the girl behind the cash register, who nodded and smiled. As he poured the hot cup of coffee, Al's mind was still gently being pulled to the recent thoughts. He basked in the afterglow and thought how exciting and wonderful life with Jesus Christ is.

At the counter he paid for the coffee and glanced at the girl, intending to make some positive comment that might lead into a statement about Jesus. Instead, he saw her wince at what seemed to be pain and asked her what the problem was. She looked at him through eyes filled with discomfort and pain and complained about the "migraine headache" that medicine didn't seem to help.

Al asked her if she knew that Jesus could heal that headache – right now?

She was plainly caught off guard at the question and

asked Al if the store manager had put him up to that just to trick her.

Al assured her that he was very serious about the question so she consented to allow him to pray for her. Very simply he reached across the counter and put his hand on her head and commanded the headache to leave "in the name of Jesus!"

And it did!

Not only did she get healed of the headache, but as Al looked on in amazement, she went down under the power of God, right there on the floor behind the cash register!

When she finally got up she was a very surprised lady. She was also a very overwhelmed lady because she knew she had been touched by God.

As Al walked out into the bright sunlight and crisp air he couldn't help but exclaim out loud, *"How great is our God"* and *"What a neat Savior we have!"*

If Grace and Al can do it, YOU can do it, too!

Chapter Two

Healing: A Life-Style

Healing is simple, easy and uncomplicated because it is all done with God's power in the name of Jesus! Healing was a life-style for Jesus and for the early disciples, and it should be exactly the same today for every born-again, Spirit-filled Christian on earth.

However, since the time when the disciples lived on earth, only a few people – mostly ministers – have been gifted with what is called a healing ministry or gifts of healing. Only recently, primarily during this generation, have ordinary Christians discovered that they, too, can do what Jesus told all of us to do.

There is a big difference between the gifts of healing and being merely obedient to the commands Jesus gave us. The gifts of healing are still present in a number of Christians, but all Christians have a responsibility to obey everything Jesus told us to do. In Mark 16:18 He said that those who believe *"will lay hands on the sick, and they will recover."* This is a life-style Jesus was talking about, not a special gift, but a normal sign and wonder that would follow every believer to confirm the fact that they were telling the truth when they spoke about His miracle-working power.

Healing is not an end unto itself, but it is a God-given tool for us to use, just as Jesus and the disciples did, so that people will believe in Jesus Christ as their Savior and Lord and be born again. It is most certainly a tool which is vitally needed by Christians today. But even more important, it is probably the best tool we have been given to aid in the evangelization of souls. When individuals are healed by the power of God, it is extremely difficult for them not to believe in Jesus.

In the beginning of our ministry, success in healing was beyond our reach because we did not have the baptism with the Holy Spirit. Our church had taught against it, and we believed it was not for today.

Because of our intense hunger, however, God opened our blinded spiritual eyes, and shortly after that we received the baptism with the Holy Spirit in an extremely exciting way. We never once questioned its reality or the fact that it was a genuine gift from God. We knew beyond all doubt that it was not just senseless jargon from the devil, as some have tried to teach.

Once we received this wonderful gift of God and spoke in tongues, we instantly knew we had received God's power within us, and we believed that every person we touched would be healed — but they weren't! We laid hands on everyone we could. More results occurred, but it was nothing like we expected, so we went back to the Bible to see how Jesus healed the sick.

As fanatical as we were about wanting to learn how to heal the sick, we never lost sight of the purpose of healing: "Jesus' disciples saw him do many other miracles besides the ones told about in this book, but these are recorded *so that you will believe that he is the Messiah, the Son of God, and that believing in him you will have life"* (John 20:30-31, TLB, italics added).

Jesus laid hands on the sick, and they recovered.

Jesus commanded fever to leave, and it obeyed.

Jesus spoke to diseases and evil spirits, and they left.

But, strangely, Jesus never "prayed" for the sick. He healed them! Paul "healed" the sick, too (Acts 28:8). A light began to shine in our hearts, and a key of understanding opened a door of healing for us.

The principle of healing the sick was summed up by Jesus as: *"The works that I do in My Father's name, they bear witness of Me. My Father, who has given them to Me, is greater than all; and no one is able to snatch them out of My Father's hand"* (John 10:25,29).

"You shall receive power when the Holy Spirit has come upon you" (Acts 1:8a).

"He who believes in Me, the works that I do he will do also; and greater works than these he will do, because I go to my Father." (John 14:12b).

We are told in the Great Commission that all these miracles are to be done in the name of Jesus. Therefore, healing is simple because it's done with the power of God's Holy Spirit and by the authority that is vested in us when we use the name of Jesus.

Let's examine the way a doctor "heals" the sick. We will assume that we have caught a germ of some kind and have made an appointment to see our doctor. He examines us and gives us his diagnosis.

Then he prescribes a certain amount of penicillin or other medication and says, "That should cause you to get over this in two or three days."

You go home, and what happens? In two or three

days you are well. Did the doctor heal you? No, he used his skill and knowledge and understanding to discover what was wrong, and he prescribed the proper medication for the problem. Did the nurse who injected the medicine heal you? No.

What healed you then? The penicillin or other prescribed medication did.

Divine healing is similar in principle. The power is injected by the laying on of hands for healing, but it is the power from the giver of power who gets all the credit.

When we receive the baptism "with" or "in" the Holy Spirit, we have the most dynamic healing power of all within us. We are endued with the power of the Holy Spirit of the Almighty God (Luke 24:49)! What an honor! What a privilege! What a responsibility! When this divine power is dispensed into a sick body, the power does the healing. We always give glory to God and Christ Jesus. Always, when ministering healing, do it in the name of Jesus.

You are a "Light Switch"

If you have ever turned a light switch on or off, you're smart enough to heal the sick!

Somewhere, not too far from where you are, is a generator (a power plant) that generates electricity. A wire brings this electricity, this power, from the source to your house and up to your electric bulb. The energy flowing from the power plant to the light bulb causes the filament of the bulb to illuminate. When this happens, we say the light is "on."

Between the power plant and the light bulb is a switch or breaker. The switch is designed to break the flow of energy, the power, from its source to the destination in the light bulb. If you turn on the switch, the two ends of the wire are connected and the energy will flow through. If it is turned off, the wires are separated, and the energy cannot continue because of the gap between the power source and the light bulb.

In the same way, the Holy Spirit in you is the generator or the power plant – the source of the power. Your hands are the on and off switch, and the person needing healing is the light bulb.

Now it is entirely up to you whether you turn the light switch on or off. It is entirely your choice in healing to lay hands on the sick. Actually, the only choice you have is whether or not you will be obedient to the command of Jesus.

The power of God will do the healing, just as the electric current will light the bulb. If you want a dark room to light up, you can turn on the light switch. If you don't flip the switch, the room will stay dark. If you have an opportunity to minister healing to someone, it is the same kind of choice. You can lay hands on them and see them recover, or you can let them remain sick.

If you have not yet received your "generator," do so right now. Ask Jesus to baptize you with the Holy Spirit. Lift your hands up to God and begin to praise Him, but not in any language you know. Start expressing sounds of love so the Holy Spirit can take whatever sounds you give Him and give you the language that will turn any ordinary individual into an extraordinary person! Let your spirit soar as it talks to God for the very first time (I Corinthians 14:2).

Be a light switch for Jesus, but be sure you are

"turned on" for Him. Jesus said, "You are the light of the world" (Matthew 5:14). Let this be part of your being the light of the world.

Laying hands on the sick and healing them is one means that Jesus used to be the light of the world, to illuminate the way for the lost to find Him. He passed this earth job on to us and gave us this healing virtue, this dynamic power, so we could effectively carry on all of His work while we are on earth.

(Charles)

Chapter Three

An Invitation To The Supernatural

The first time we ever saw Diana Radabaugh was at a Healing Explosion. The minute we met her we saw the anointing of God and we saw the potential in her. We tried to help her develop but she was a very bashful housewife and we had difficulty ever getting her to the front of an auditorium! Every time we would spot her coming in we would call her up because we knew that here was a woman called and anointed by God for a very special ministry.

As you read her story, you might discover that you think you are exactly the same as she was, an "ordinary" person.....read on and discover how God can use such a person in an extraordinary way!

I tell you this with the greatest of confidence; if you will but launch out into the depth of your life with the Lord, He will show you that you, *your life,* can count greatly for His glory, honor and holy praise.

God's Word says, *"Do not be overcome by evil, but overcome evil with good."* I want to include this with my story because it is important to some who, while reading this testimony, are in the middle of a great trial. Thinking God has forgotten you, or believing the enemy's lies that you're incapable of being anything but defeated in your life.

In the middle of the greatest travesty of my life I received a little white post card, inviting me to a luncheon in Indianapolis given by Charles and Frances Hunter. This was over three hours by car from our home. I was despondent and depressed from a savage attack by the enemy on our family. Though I didn't understand why at the time, I decided that I would accept the Hunters' invitation.

Sometimes when we are totally surrendered to the Lord at the most unusual times, He brings into our lives, the greatest adventures we could ever imagine. That was exactly what He was about to do in mine.

As I walked up the stairs, Bob Barker, the Hunter's son-in-law, seeing me, said, "Now there is an evangelist, if I've ever seen one." Those words were prophetic, and to be honest I didn't even know what prophetic meant at the time. I was an honest Baptist gal saved sixteen years, sharing Jesus with whomever I could. I was just Jerry's wife, and the mother of Tina, Jerry, Jr. and Tim; just a housewife from Elkhart, Indiana. God was about to introduce me to a dynamic whirlwind escapade, via Charles and Frances Hunter.

As one of the Hunters' staff put the promotional tape on the big screen, I watched in absolute awe, as they showed people being prayed for by Charles and Frances. The people were falling out in the Spirit. I watched in utter amazement as legs appeared to grow out. People were giving testimony of their backs being healed. Over the past several years, I had back problems. I couldn't help wondering if God would do that healing for me.

The complete excitement I felt coming off that tape

electrified the entire room. I fell totally and madly in love with that outrageously precious couple on the tape. Until this moment, I had only heard their names through my friend Beverly, who had shared some of their books with me. The energy and explosive faith they showed really excited me. Tears flowed as I watched the humble testimonies of people who had been held captive in physical torment by the enemy and yet one touch of Jesus through Charles or Frances, and they were set absolutely free.

Each time I heard Frances say, "If Charles and Frances can do it, you can do it too," it somehow seemed to echo deep into my heart. When I heard Charles say, "What do you have to lose?" I wondered...what DID I have to lose?

It was then I heard the captain of my soul whisper my name, and tell me that He wanted me to accept the challenge that was being offered; He wanted me to teach the course, "How To Heal The Sick." After all, if Charles and Frances can do it, I could do it too!...Frances promised...!!

As I left that life-inspiring meeting, my mind was spinning during the drive home. I prayed, "Oh God, I will do this because You have told me to, but how? Who will I get to come to these meetings? I've never taught anyone but four-year-olds in Sunday School." I had a million questions for Him; He had a million and one answers for me.

The first meeting was in my home, eight weeks after my encounter with the Hunters via video in Indianapolis. Twelve people came. I'll never forget the first time people came up to me for prayer. Untrained, unskilled, just a housewife, dependent only on Jesus Christ to make good His Word, and that He did. Each week was more exciting than the last; people were being healed!

The tape would be shown with Charles and Frances, "How To Heal The Sick." Then I would instruct the students where to place their thumbs as they put them on the ankle bones; how to do the neck thing, and all the other wonderful things taught.

The Lord was my teacher and He knows I called on Him over and over again, never trusting myself, because I really knew very little. I would rely on the Holy Spirit for whatever was needed at this time and situation.

I'll never forget a lady coming up to me with a migraine headache; she had been in pain many days, violently ill. When I laid my hands on her head to make the command for the pain to go, in Jesus name, the Lord showed me a vision of her heart. I could see the large artery was blocked and the blood was barely getting through. Immediately, I spoke to that condition in the name of Jesus. She started sobbing and fell out in the Spirit. I continued to pray for others. Soon I felt a tug on my sleeve. The lady that I had prayed for stood weeping, saying how did you know that I had a heart problem? I am scheduled for surgery on Monday morning. I know that I am healed; look, my circulation is working; my hands are warm. I can feel my feet! I just simply told her that I didn't know about her heart, but that Jesus did and He wanted her healed. We hugged and rejoiced in the great mercy and tremendous healing power of Jesus.

After several weeks of class the final night came. We all had grown so much in the knowledge of the Word of God and His ways. It was hard thinking it was all over. For some reason, I thought it would all end. ...After all, I had taught the course like the Lord said. I felt like I'd found an answer to the fulfillment of life serving the Lord and His people...yet now it was over!

Then two days later, I received an invitation to come and teach at a home in South Bend. After that I was invited to teach a class at The Christian Center, under Dr. Lester Sumrall. After that, a school run by Catholic nuns in Fort Wayne. Then the Honeywell Center, and a class for the Full Gospel Businessmen in Wabash, Indiana. Another home and another church, in the northern corner of Indiana. At one time I had five classes going at the same time. Oh how exciting...Jesus Christ, the same yesterday, today, and forever. The signs; the wonders; the miracles... "Because He Lives."

The Hunters had put out their tabloid telling of an upcoming Healing Explosion in Indianapolis, at the Hoosier Dome. This was a huge 10,000 people crusade. Life and hope, salvations, deliverances, healings. It was as if Heaven came down and Glory filled the stadium. Many of the students of the course, "How To Heal The Sick," that I had instructed, had come to that great meeting.

Charles and Frances were even more dynamic and powerful in person. I wanted to just stand and watch the Lord work through them, but having been put on a healing team myself, I had to get about my Father's business.

I had promised Marty, (a lady I had taught at Calvary Temple in Fort Wayne), that if she would make the effort and come to the Healing Explosion, I would be her partner. Marty was so shy, even though she came, she kept quoting things the Hunters had said in the videos. Then she started quoting me in some of the encouragements that I had given to her, encouraging her faith. She started pleading with me NOT to let her pray for the people. "After all, you are the teacher, you pray for them, I'll just stand beside the people and pray in the Spirit." I reassured her Jesus wanted to use her also. Not just me. He needs us all.

The healing teams were lined up two by two. When someone said from the platform, "Teams, take your positions"...and "Oh, yes, we need a couple more over in the Wheel Chair Section," Marty jumped to her feet, grabbed my arm, pulled me up and started squealing.

"Come on! Let's go! That's us!" ... "That's us?" I said. "What's us?" "Come on, we're going over to the Wheel Chair Section." Even though I had instructed many classes by now, I wasn't sure that I wanted to be put loose in the wheel chair section.

The next thing I know, I'm standing, looking down on a lady who told us that she had every disease known to man, who had been in the wheel chair for twelve years. I looked over at Marty, confidently looking at me as if to say, "Well, come on, let's get to praying."

I had heard on that tape of "How To Heal The Sick" Frances telling the story of someone whose faith went right down through their toes; at this moment I knew exactly what that felt like. Marty and I laid hands on the lady. I was not feeling a thing at the moment but I was thinking...why did I ask Marty to be my partner? I concluded the command "In Jesus name." The lady said, "Look, I can wiggle my right big toe; I haven't done that in years." Feeling excited for her excitement, I couldn't help but think there was a whole lot left to do.

We pressed through and Agnus kept receiving miracles, one by one. First her migraine left, then her paralyzed hand and arm started to move after we cast out the spirit of death. Then she felt the burning of her ulcer leave. Before it was all over she really did receive a "complete overhaul."

Jesus Christ, true to His Word, healed her everywhere. She was the only one we worked with at that Crusade. It was worth it because she came as a living dead person and the last we saw her, she was pushing her wheel chair with her two grandsons at her side. We were waving good-bye to each other. I could not think of when I loved my Jesus more, making Agnus whole and healthy to have quality life to share with her grandbabies. I've kept in contact with her through the years and she is still walking in victory.

When the Louisville Kentucky Healing Explosion happened, being in the presence of the great anointing Charles and Frances carried, you could not help but know God was tremendously using these dedicated people. They kept telling you with all confidence that the Lord wanted to use ALL of us.

As their testimony goes, the Lord told them one day, after asking Him why He chose them, His reply was, "Because you're dumb enough to do what I tell you to do!" I too felt that was me. If the Lord said it would happen, who am I to tell the God of the universe it wouldn't. So I felt really, really excited when the Lord dropped into my spirit to have my own hometown Healing Explosion. After all, what did I have to lose?...

Oh my, it was so much work with no one in the beginning catching the vision. I asked my beloved husband Jerry, who at this point was still very "Baptist," in his belief, if I could have this healing explosion in his 40' x 60' truck garage. He almost hysterically said "Sure." This garage had seven inches of grease on the floor, tools and truck parts all over. What could you do? What could come out of this ugliness?

Jerry let me start with one bay of the three bay garage. I cleaned and scrubbed and prayed. God sent one older man who got the vision and he and I went to work getting so much done it was incredible because the Lord was on our side. Before all was done, someone donated a huge piece of carpet to hang as a back drop. Someone else borrowed a platform and chairs from their church. Jerry seeing the transformation and the determination started moving the big equipment around helping wherever he could. Others caught the vision. We had the most anointed praise and worship team and prayer intercessors come on board to bring this vision to pass. Our first Healing Explosion brought one hundred people out. It was a glorious success, all to our Lord God's glory. Several received Jesus as Savior, there were awesome healings and God even sent us some angels whom a couple of people had seen, even my mother.

So many wonderful stories of so many beautiful people. And of course, the overwhelming miracles that I have been a part of is (Charles says it best), "What good will it do if you get someone healed and they die and go to hell, healed?" Healing is a tool Jesus Himself uses to draw people.

As I now have the great privilege and honor to travel internationally with Charles and Frances, and get to be a part of their 40,000 to 60,000 people crusades, I get to see the greatest miracle of all as Charles and Frances throw out the lifeline to thousands of people in the U.S. as well as over all the world. I see people receive and accept the Lord Jesus Christ. I have worked with them and have been used in the vision the Lord gave Charles on taking a census of the world.

As I and a few other Americans went with them to Honduras we joined with a great number of the nationals and saw in a couple of weeks, one million people say "YES" to the call of salvation as we presented the gospel door to door. In America I was able to coordinate the state of Indiana for the National Evangelistic Census.

God has blessed me with the great privilege of producing my own television program called "Miracles." This is a weekly one-hour program and we've been on the air for five years. We opened the "Because He Lives Ministry Center" to accommodate the "How To Heal The Sick" classes and to host our version of Healing Explosions, which we call "A Night Of Miracles." My husband and I have worked in this labor of love for two years. Now God has given us the vision of building a beautiful anointed ministry center in Elkhart, Indiana.

In this period of time I have been ordained with and by Dr. Lester Sumrall 1990...because I said "YES, Lord, here I am...Send me even in the middle of a disaster." God can and will make a way for you if you will only reach out and give Him your all, for His glory!!

He might even send to you a couple of earthly angels to tell you, "If they can do it, YOU can do it too. What do you have to lose?"

Diana Radabaugh

Chapter Four

The Immune System

You will be used in many healings because you know to what part of the body you should direct God's power in Jesus' name. To minister effectively, you will also need to understand the importance of a healthy, active immune system.

In the Chinese world there are two written languages, the complex and the simplex, and both of them are exactly what their names imply – one is complicated and the other is simple.

The original written Chinese language, regardless of which dialect you speak, is always the same. The original complex requires a tremendous number of strokes to make every letter and is still used by the older people in all of the Chinese speaking nations today. However, we don't know the history behind it, but the younger generation decided they wanted a more simplified way to write and so they made up the simplified Chinese alphabet which takes a small percentage of the strokes of the original language and which is written and read much faster by those who know the language.

There are two ways to describe healing, one is the compex way and the other is the simplex way. God has really spoken to us and told us to make healing simple and to teach it so that people will understand that healing is a natural life-style for Christians. That is what we will try to do in this book.

We have two descriptions of the immune system, the simplex and the complex and we decided to give you the simplex first.

The immune system is that part of your body which sets up the smoke screen so that disease cannot come in and tear your body down. The immune system is protected by taking care of yourself, by seeing that you get enough sleep, by seeing that you get enough rest and by seeing that you don't over extend yourself in any area.

You may remember when you were young that your mother gave you instructions to be careful and get enough sleep, to be careful and keep yourself warm on cold days, to be sure and not over extend yourself because she would say, "If you do, your system will get 'run down' and you'll catch a cold." What your mother was really saying was, "Take care of your immune system the proper way and you won't catch cold so easily."

With all the interest in proper eating and vitamins, which is greater today than at any time either of us remember, it doesn't hurt anybody to take Vitamin C to help keep your immune system up. If we will do just a few things like that, it will help tremendously to keep our bodies strong so that the warriors that we have in the immune system will be strong and will be able to fight off anything with which we are attacked. Drink enough fresh orange juice and other juices and eat the right kind of balanced meals instead of those fast foods, fried meals all the time. Drink lots of water every day. We both also take liquid minerals every day.

We know that you have seen many people who seem to walk through an epidemic of flu, or any other diseases and never seem to "catch" anything. This is because they have a strong immune system. The immune system is vital to keep us healthy, that's why it's so simple to pray and say, "In the name of Jesus I command a new immune system into myself." Then believing that you have received it, take care of it and see how much less sickness you have.

That's the simple version of the immune system and yet there are people who like a medical explanation, so here's the medical explanation for you.

The following is a quote from the Complete Home Medical Guide (Columbia University College of Physicians and Surgeons, Crown Publishers Inc., New York).

"To understand allergies, one must first understand the immune system, whose misdirected response causes allergic reactions. The job of the immune system is to search for, recognize, and destroy germs and other dangerous invaders of the body, known as antigens. It does this by producing antibodies or special molecules to match and counteract each antigen.

"The key soldiers of the immune system are the lymphocytes, the white blood cells manufactured by the millions in the bone marrow. The lymphocytes produce antibodies specific to each unwanted antigen. Circulating in the bloodstream, the antibodies attack the antigen, or protect the body's cells from invasion by the antigen, or make the invader palatable to roaming scavenger cells called macrophages. Antibody-producing lymphocytes or plasma cells are called "B" cells.

"When lymphocytes are activated, some of them become 'memory' cells. Then the next time a person encounters that same antigen which earlier turned the lymphocytes on, the immune system 'remembers' it and is primed to destroy it immediately. This is acquired immunity."

Apparently the immune system ignores cancer cells until they spread cancer. This may also be true of AIDS or other mysterious diseases for which science has found no cure. But doctors and scientists believe they may have discovered a way to develop an immunity to cancer cells.

We are now testing a new area of commands for cancer patients, saying, "In Jesus' name, we command the memory of the immune system to be healed, so that it recognizes and destroys the invading cancer cells."

Because of the importance of the immune system in every disease that attacks our bodies, it never hurts to command a new immune system to come into an individual. Remember that you can do absolutely no harm to someone by commanding a new immune system.

If you feel like you are "catching a cold," command your immune system to be made healthy and new. The immune system is so vital to every part of our life that we cannot overprotect it.

Chapter Five

The Spine

It is estimated that close to 80 percent of adults have back and/or neck problems of some sort. Most of these problems are a result of some type of injury. Usually the condition that occurs is a combination of misaligned vertebrae, muscle strain, ligament and tendon strain or tearing. The discs that sit between the vertebrae may also be damaged.

With such a high incidence of spinal problems, a large percentage of people need to be healed of back and/or neck problems. Charles and Frances have nicknamed ways of ministering healing to these injuries:

The neck thing
The pelvic thing
Growing out arms
Growing out legs

They call the combination of all of these "the total thing." Therefore we will briefly review the spine and its problems.

The vertebrae are the bones that make up the spinal column. They sit one on top of the other. In between these vertebrae are the discs, or pads, that allow a certain amount of motion in bending and twisting the back and neck. All of these bones are held in place by sets of ligaments, tendons and muscles. In a person's back, the vertebral column is a channel made up of the circular rings of bone on the back of the vertebrae. This channel houses and protects the spinal cord, the main bundle of nerves running from the brain to all the parts of the body.

A severe fracture or dislocation can cause damage to the cord itself or to any of the thirty-one pairs of nerve roots that come out from between the individual vertebrae. Damage to a disc, which is the pad between the vertebrae, can cause it to bulge out and put pressure on a nerve root. This creates pain and, at times, weakness on either one side or both sides of the body.

Figure I at the end of this chapter describes which ailments are associated with disorders in each section of the spine.

The portion of the spine located under the base of the skull is called the cervical spine. This series is made up of the first seven vertebrae, the topmost being the atlas and the second one the axis. The head rotates from side to side on the atlas, and forward and backward on the axis.

The nerves from the cervical spine affect the face and the head, the neck, the shoulders and down the arms. Any pressure on these nerves will cause pain and interference with normal functioning in these areas. For healing in this area Charles and Frances do "the neck thing."

The thoracic (or dorsal) spine consists of the next twelve vertebrae, each of which has a pair of ribs coming off the sides, forming the rib cage. The nerves that come out from the spinal cord at this level affect the lower arms, the hands and the chest. For healing in this area they do what is called "growing out arms."

The lumbar spine consists of the bottom five vertebrae, where the nerves supplying the legs and feet come from between the vertebrae. For healing in this area they do what is called "growing out legs."

The next bone, rather larger than the vertebrae, is called the sacrum. It supplies support for the entire spinal column. The sacrum is also joined to the two hip, or iliac, bones (part of the pelvis) through a series of ligaments, tendons and the sacroiliac joints. Just below the sacrum is the coccyx bone, a short bone that comes close to the rectum, also known as the tail bone. For ministering healing to the entire pelvic area, Charles and Frances do what is called "the pelvic thing."

While ministering to someone with a neck or back injury, do not remove or readjust an orthopedic apparatus. To do so is illegal unless you are a licensed medical professional.

After the person has been ministered to, the Hunters suggest that you ask whether the pain is gone while the collar or brace is still in place. He or she may want to remove the apparatus to see what God has done. Let it be the individual's choice whether or not to do so.

Encourage the person to return to his or her doctor for evaluation, qualification or verification as appropriate.

(Dr. Roy J. LeRoy)

*Note: Dr. Roy J. LeRoy has been to almost all of our Healing Explosions. He is an outstanding chiropractor who practiced in his field for forty years before he retired. Now he shares his valuable knowledge and experience with the body of Christ.

FIGURE 1

TO ALL SECTIONS OF THE HEAD AND FACE
TO THROAT
TO UPPER LIMBS
TO HEART
TO LUNGS
TO GALL BLADDER
TO STOMACH
TO LIVER
TO KIDNEYS
TO INTESTINES
TO APPENDIX
TO BOWELS
TO GENITALS
TO BLADDER
TO LOWER LIMBS

1. Dizziness, headaches, nervousness, eye and ear problems, high blood pressure, chronic tiredness, migraine headaches, nervous breakdown, insomnia, fainting spells, glandular troubles, allergy.

2. Skin disorders, hay fever, wry or stiff neck, neuralgia, neuritis, sore throat hoarseness.

3. Bronchial conditions, throat conditions, arm and shoulder pain, bursitis, asthma, coughs, thyroid conditions.

4. Pain and numbness in forearms and hands, chest pains, congestion, palpitation, "nervous" or fast heart, pleurisy.

5. Gall bladder problems, jaundice, shingles, stomach upsets, heart-burn, fever.

6. Low blood pressure, poor circulation, ulcers, hives, stomach trouble.

7. Hiccoughs, lowered resistance, dyspepsia, circulatory problems, rheumatism.

8. Certain types of sterility, impotence, menstrual troubles, diarrhea, constipation.

9. Knee pain, varicose veins, prostate problems, bed wetting, backaches, cold feet.

10. Poor circulation, leg cramps, hemorrhoids, ankle swelling, rectal itching, pain on sitting.

44

Chapter Six

The Neck Thing

We decided in the beginning of our ministry that God had made everything simple and therefore we should too. So we gave simple titles to all the things we do in healing to make them easy to identify and store away in your memory file. God enlightened us about "the neck thing" a long time ago.

We had a guest in our home who had a pain in his toe. I "grew out" his arms and legs, and the pain did not leave. So I asked the guest what the doctor said was causing the pain. I did this because we believe that if you don't get healed by divine power, you should see a doctor to find out what the problem is. Then we can know where and how to minister healing by God's power.

He said the chiropractor had told him that he had a thin disc in his back. Although the thin disc was in the lower back, the doctor "adjusted" the man's neck. This relieved the pain, but subsequently it returned.

In accordance with Mark 16 *("Those who believe... will lay hands on the sick..." vv. 17-18)*, I put my two hands on his neck, placing my fingers on his upper spinal column. I did not realize where the other parts of my hands were actually resting. Later I discovered that the palms of my hands were on the carotid arteries, the main arteries on both sides of the neck that supplies blood to the brain. My palms were also on the nerves that go from the brain down the front of your body.

This hand position automatically makes your thumbs fall right on the temporomandibular joint, better known as TMJ. I was laying hands (thumbs) on one of the strongest muscles of the body. Was it accidental that God made our hands so that when we placed them in the right position we would be "laying hands" on three vital parts of the body at one time? Or did He plan it so that when we started probing into how to heal the sick the supernatural way, we would discover what He knew all along?

With my hands gently in place as described above, I then asked the man to turn his face slowly to the left and then to the right, then backward and forward.

Then I asked him to rotate his head. At the same time I was doing what we later named "the neck thing": I commanded all the muscles, ligaments, tendons, nerves, discs and vertebrae to go into place, and the thin disc to be healed in the name of Jesus.

When he rotated his head, he shouted, "The pain is gone!"

We used this technique for years and discovered the results were also phenomenal for headaches. Then one day Dr. LeRoy told us what we were actually doing and why the results were so tremendous.

We have seen outstanding healings through the neck thing, not only in our ministry, but also through the hundreds of thousands who have learned this supernatural application of God's healing power through our healing seminars, healing explosions, video/audio tapes and books.

Almost one hundred percent of neck problems; headaches; nerve deafness; arthritis in the neck; fractured vertebrae; deteriorated, herniated and disintegrated discs; and even broken necks and problems with TMJ have been healed by this application of God's healing power.

Large percentages of health problems will be healed through the basic healing application of the total thing, growing out arms and legs, the neck thing and the pelvic thing. This healing affects not only the spinal system but also internal parts, because nerves make muscles work properly.

(Charles)

The Sciatica or the Sciatic Nerve

Did you ever have a pain shoot down your entire leg, and you felt as if your leg was going to buckle under you? You were probably a victim of sciatica, a painful situation generally caused by a pinched nerve. This is usually caused when a disc wears thin on one side. When that happens, the spine tips on the side where the thinning disc has occurred and causes the body to put pressure on the sciatic nerve which causes the pain to then shoot down the leg. Normally this happens only on one side or the other, depending on where the thinning has occurred. It can also be caused by a strained back but normally it comes from a nerve that has been pinched.

This is one of the most painful of back problems, but one of the easiest to heal. It is very easy to find the exact spot once you learn where to place two fingers, because the area is always very painful and sensitive to touch. Once you discover how to locate the junction of the pelvic bone and the sacrum, lay two fingers on the area of the back (on the side where the problem is) and command the spirit of sciatica to come out in the name of Jesus. Have the person bend over. It is when the person bends over and puts their faith into action that the healing actually occurs.

In almost all cases, the minute they bend over and put their faith into action after you touched that sacroiliac joint, the pressure will be relieved and the person will be healed. If you will look at the diagram below, you will see exactly where the sacroiliac joint is located and it's very easy to learn exactly where to put your fingers on one side or the other. If you can imagine one of the discs being thin and the spine bending one way or the other, you will see why there will be a "pinch" in that area.

Recently an administrator of a church came to me when the service was over and said, "I can hardly walk. This pain shoots down my leg to my toe, and it's killing me!" I placed my fingers on her sciatic nerve. Before I said a word, the power of God had healed her. Laughing, she said, "It's gone!"

(Frances)

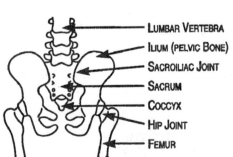

LUMBAR VERTEBRA
ILIUM (PELVIC BONE)
SACROILIAC JOINT
SACRUM
COCCYX
HIP JOINT
FEMUR

The sacroiliac can assume many different positions. Sometimes the ilium (pelvic bone) rotates on the sacrum and causes one leg to appear short. Or it can go out of position, causing the spine to be crooked (scoliosis) even though the legs appear to be even. The sacrum can tilt forward and cause lordosis Q.24 (swayback), or backward and cause a straight "military" back. In all these examples, do the pelvic thing (Chapter 7) and command the sacrum to move into correct position.

Chapter Seven

The Pelvic Thing

God will give you "witty inventions" and ideas beyond your ability and capability if you will be sensitive to the Holy Spirit and move when He moves.

At a service in Jacksonville, Florida, a man who was duck-footed, with his feet pointed outward, came forward. I certainly didn't know what to pray except to command his feet to turn inward instead of outward.

But then a thought flashed through my mind. It seemed as if God was indicating it had something to do with the spine. I asked a chiropractor who was with us whether there could be a problem in the spine that could cause the man's feet to turn out.

The chiropractor replied that the man's pelvic bones were turned out and needed to be turned inward. In the natural realm, or even in the scope of chiropractic treatment, this would be difficult or impossible to do, but in God's kingdom and in the supernatural world it's no problem.

I placed my hands on the top of his pelvic bones and commanded the pelvis to rotate inward until his feet were normal. I was probably the most surprised person there when I noticed the entire pelvic area turn from side to side.

I wasn't doing it.

He wasn't doing it.

It had to be the power of God!

Just as quickly as the rotating had started, it stopped. The man fell under the power of God. When he stood up again, his feet were no longer turned outward; they were perfectly straight. Once again God had opened a natural-supernatural channel for us to learn more about healing.

It didn't take us long to figure out that if rotating in with the power of God would correct feet which turned out, then surely rotating out would correct feet that are pigeon-toed or turned inward. We tried it, and it worked. Since then we have seen many people healed of feet that turn in.

We've discussed this healing technique with many doctors on our doctors' panels. They've all agreed it could be invaluable in the healing of many other diseases as well. Because of the involvement of the entire pelvic area, many female problems are healed through the simple laying on of hands. Hundreds of women have been healed of premenstrual syndrome by the simple act of commanding the female organs to go into place and be healed while the pelvis is rotating.

Many problems in the lower lumbar area (the lower five vertebrae) and the sacrum are healed by commanding the vertebrae to be adjusted properly. Often a frozen or dislocated sacrum is restored to its right position by doing the pelvic thing.

Further, prostate problems often can be healed this way by commanding the prostate to become normal.

Colon problems are healed by commanding nerves controlling the colon to become normal. Any organ or part of the body which lies between the waistline and the hips can often be healed by this simple act.

It never hurts to look at a picture of the human body so you will know where certain parts are located. The pelvic bones are sometimes called the hip bones. They are the flat bones that make up your skeletal structure for the hip and pelvic area. If you will run your hands down your side in the area of your waist, you will discover that the top of the bones lie right in that area. That is where you place your fingers when you command healing.

Once you give a command in the name of Jesus, the pelvis will rotate or move in one direction or the other – if that portion of the body needs adjusting. If nothing is needed, nothing will happen, and the pelvis will not move.

If one side of the pelvis is higher than the other, command the high side to lower and the low side to come up. Don't underestimate the value of this simple healing process. The results are incredible.

(Frances)

Chapter Eight

Supernatural "Foote" Steps

We met Andrew Foote through a healing explosion which he attended because his brother shocked him as he told Andrew of the incredible things that happened at "those kind of meetings." He had always had a hunger to heal the sick and at the time he came to us he was a handsome young bachelor. Because of being so handsome he had a lot of girls running after him. However, he was so intent on learning how to heal the sick that none of this made any difference to him.

Today he is the handsome father of five beautiful children, having prayed himself in a beautiful godly wife. This has never taken away his love of healing the sick and preaching the gospel.

All of these stories are completely different, told by different people in different areas of life but they all lead to the same focal point. We know you will enjoy Andrew's story.

Since I was a young boy, I've wanted to see others made well but the only way I knew how to participate in that process was to become a medical doctor. The medical profession therefore became my pursuit but things didn't go quite the way I had planned. After eight years of pursuing my goal between college and work in the medical profession, during which time numerous medical school applications with adequate requirements were declined, I became discouraged and chose a longtime hobby for a profession instead.

Four years later though, in March of 1986, those childhood desires were rekindled when my older brother shared with me his experience at a Healing Explosion held by Charles and Frances Hunter. What he told me was a little hard to believe so I decided to attend the next Healing Explosion in Detroit, Michigan to experience for myself what he had.

In order to know for certain what my brother had told me was true, I took a friend with me who was ill with stomach ulcers, bleeding hemorrhoids and a badly sprained elbow. To my utter astonishment, when a couple of ordinary believers laid hands on my friend and prayed in the name of Jesus, he was completely healed!

That was the turning point of my life because now knowing that God was real, I surrendered my life to Him. I realized that if God had kept me alive and cared for me all those years I had run from Him in disobedience how much more would He take care of me and fulfill my heart's desires if I put my life in His hands.

I had always desired to be used by God in some way, but could He and would He was the question. Seeing that the Lord had just used two ordinary people like me to heal my friend, I now knew He could. But whether He would was still unanswered. I certainly hadn't lived a life worthy of His use. There was only one way I knew of to answer that question and that was to learn what these people had learned whom God had used so powerfully at the Healing Explosion.

I began attending a Hunter Video Healing School at a local church and it was there I received the baptism of the Holy Spirit and spoke in tongues for the first time. I was still a little apprehensive because this was all new to me so I sat in the back of the class where I could just sit and observe.

During one of the training sessions our instructor asked for those in the class who had pain or sickness in their body to come to the front of the class. About twenty of the one hundred students made their way to the front. Then he asked for volunteers to come minister to the sick but only about five people volunteered. So he began picking volunteers and for some strange reason, out of everyone, he started with me sitting all the way in the back of the room.

To be honest, I was nervous and scared. What if God didn't heal the person I prayed for? I'd look like an idiot in front of everyone. Well, this was the moment of truth and at this point I'd look more like an idiot if I didn't go and pray for someone.

I then walked up to a woman and asked her what she needed prayer for. She responded by saying she had a pinched nerve in her neck, tightness in her shoulders and had numerous headaches. I ministered to her as Charles and Frances had taught on their training video and as I looked up at her face, she had tears running down her cheeks. My first thought was maybe I had somehow hurt her but she told me her pain was all gone.

I don't think I'd ever been more excited about anything in my life. By one act of grace, God not only answered the question of whether He would use me but also fulfilled a childhood desire of mine to see others made well. The Lord had truly put my past behind me but I realized I needed to do the same. From this point in time I had no other desire greater than doing what was pleasing to the Lord. His love and mercy extended to me by no act of my own, made me want to love and serve Him all the more.

God began to open my eyes to how many hurting people we pass by on a daily basis but being so busy with our own lives we hardly even notice. As He placed various people in my path it became quite obvious He wanted me to pray for them and to my amazement, nearly every one who would allow me to minister to them was healed. God was demonstrating His reality to each one of these people just as He had done for me. But it was up to me to open my mouth so that's what I determined to do.

As owner and operator of an automotive paint and body shop, I had numerous opportunities at work to minister to customers who were injured in their car wreck as well as salesmen coming to the shop to sell anything from tools to insurance.

As I began to share my testimony with them and how God still heals today, they would tell me of their physical ailments and the majority were healed and their lives changed by the power of God and the revelation that the same God that just healed their bodies could save their soul.

In order to learn more about ministering healing I began traveling to many other Healing Explosions and various services that Charles and Frances held. I took along my camera initially to take pictures to show some skeptical friends but later it developed into a service for the Hunters' tabloids. At one of the services, Frances asked me to minister healing to a young man who was suffering from extreme headaches. After ministering to him, he rejoiced claiming his headache was completely gone. Being extremely grateful we hugged and said good-bye.

I didn't give it another thought until a year later when our paths crossed again at a service held by the Power Team. There he told me about the state of his condition the night I had prayed for him. He had had a headache for ten months with no relief. Doctors had given him every pain-killing drug possible but none relieved his pain. A neurosurgeon had even done surgery in his neck to burn the nerves going to the area of pain in his head but that had only left him with the back of his neck numb. He was at the end of his rope when he came to the service that night. He planned on committing suicide that night when he returned home if he wasn't healed.

He told me he was quite disappointed when I was asked to pray for him instead of Frances but God healed him anyway, not only removing his headache for the first time in ten months but also totally restoring the nerves in the back of his neck. He said my hand was the first thing he'd felt on the back of his neck since the surgery. His life was never the same after that night.

He surrendered his life to Jesus Christ and a short time later purchased the HOW TO HEAL THE SICK video tapes. After learning how to minister to the sick he began to boldly minister wherever he went, healing the sick and leading people to Jesus. He became one of the greatest soulwinners I've ever known. What an incredible transformation, from a man ready to end his own life to one out changing others lives. We may never know how serious a condition others lives are in but if we'll reach out with a healing hand, it may just be the rope that saves their life as well as their soul.

Andrew Foote

Chapter Nine

Growing Out Arms And Legs Isn't Really Growing Out Arms And Legs!

If you have never seen an arm or a leg "grow out" you are in for a real treat! Of all the miracles we have seen accomplished in our services, there are two that are remembered more than any other. One is when an arm grows out and the other is when a leg grows out. It is an interesting thing to note in our mail that comes in or comments from people whom we see at other services, the greatest thing they remember is, "I saw my own arm grow out," or "I saw my leg grow out."

Watching the power of God move a part of the body right in front of your own eyes is an awesome miracle to see. It is also perhaps the simplest and most commonly performed and it is also a tremendous way to convince someone who is unsaved or not yet filled with the Spirit of the power of a living God who heals the sick.

The spine is divided into three sections, the top seven vertebrae are called cervical vertebrae or the vertebrae of the neck. The next twelve below that are the thoracic or dorsal vertebrae and each of these is hooked to a pair of ribs. The third section is the lumbar which is the lower five and this is where lower back problems occur which are the most common of all injuries for the very simple reason that we use our lower back for lifting, for bending, and for many other purposes, therefore it runs into problems more often than any other part of the body.

Probably the second part where we develop problems is in the neck and once again this is for the same reason. Neither the top five nor the lower seven vertebrae and disc have any support as the thoracic do in the way of ribs so it's much easier, since they do not have support, for them to get out of line or to be injured.

The neck is used in many different areas and is used a greater portion of the time probably than any other part of the back. Your head is constantly turning so that you can see what you need to see. If you're driving, your neck is constantly turning so it is very easy for the neck to get out of position.

To heal the neck, you can do "The Neck Thing" (see Chapter 5) and the middle back or the thoracic area is something you might want to try on yourself.

Stand up straight, put your feet together so that your toes are even and look straight ahead so that your toes and your nose are in the same direction. Extend your arms in front of you with the palms facing each other, about a half-inch apart. Then push or stretch your arms straight out as far as you can. This exercise will help you test for spinal problems in the upper part of your back.

While your arms are stretched, bring your hands tightly together. Hold them together until you bend your elbows so that you can see the ends of your fingers.

If you have a spinal problem in the thoracic or middle part of your back, the fingers on one arm will come out farther than the fingers on the other. This is normally not because your arm is short but because your back is out of alignment. If this is the case with you, then you have an opportunity to see a miracle. Stretch your arms out in front of you again, letting your hands touch each other lightly, but don't hold them tightly together.

You might want to say something like this, "Spine, in the name of Jesus, I command you to be healed. Muscles, nerves, ligaments and tendons, be adjusted in the name of Jesus." Using your knowledge of the problem, command healing as specifically as you can. Then give thanks to Jesus and believe it is done. Stand there for a few moments, and watch the miracle as the arm grows....and it will grow!

Right in front of your very own eyes you will see the short arm grow to the length of the other arm. Just seeing it even up will do something to you! You might even feel the adjustment! The adjustment, however, will be either in the back or the neck, wherever the problem happens to be, not in your arms.

Lower back problems are easy to locate because 80% of the world's population have a back problem of one kind or another and it seems the lower back is where you can get the most remarkable healings. Recently a man came to us who had fallen off a three story building thirteen years before, injuring his back, and had been unable to work for thirteen whole years. He was instantly healed when his leg grew out. It was not the leg growing out, it was the back going into position which then made the leg appear to grow out because most of the time the legs are actually not short. The way this man rejoiced was absolutely unbelievable. He jumped up and down, bent over, ran, walked up and down stairs, did everything that he had been unable to do for thirteen years and what rejoicing there was. The procedure for growing out legs is very easy.

The person to be healed should sit erect in a straight-backed chair with his or her hips positioned tightly against the back of the chair. You should be standing in front of him or her. The person should extend the legs parallel to the floor without forcing the legs to stretch beyond the point of pain. Hold the person's ankles so that the inside tips of your thumbs are exactly on top of the peak of the inside ankle bones on both legs. Thumbs should be directly opposite each other and pointed straight at the floor. This allows you to help support the uplifted legs.

Remember the person's specific problem, and command the answer to the problem. Don't just command the leg to grow, but command the problem to be corrected, whether it is from an automobile accident, crushed discs, deterioration, scoliosis or whatever.

Command it to be corrected in the name of Jesus.

The most important part of this particular healing takes place in the next few seconds. Tell the person to stand up and bend over or do something that they could not do up until this time. Again, this is when you put your faith into action that the miracle occurs. Many times a person with this sort of a problem will have a "pop" occur in their back when they bend over. That is always the time for rejoicing because that often signals a healing has been accomplished.

Recently a woman came to one of our services who was in such excruciating pain you could see it in her face and actually her entire body because of the way she walked and the way she held her shoulders.

She had been in an automobile accident 36 years

prior to this and the doctors said the accident had dis-lodged almost every vertebrae and disc in her back. She said, "I have not lived for 36 years. I have only existed because of the pain which I cannot stand." She said she had been to every doctor, every chiropractor, every medical clinic she could find and no one had been able to give her any relief whatsoever.

We did two things on her, "The Leg Thing" and "The NUCCA" (Chapter 14) and the woman was instantly and totally healed. Frances was sitting where she could see the expression on the woman's face as her leg grew out and she said it would have been wonderful if we could have had a video of that so that the world could see what happened to that woman in just the twinkling of an eye. As she saw her leg appear to grow out her eyes got wider and wider and wider with almost unbelief, "I can't believe this is happening to me," and yet the joy on her face was telling us that the nerves and muscles or whatever had been bound up had been released in the name of Jesus!

This particular miracle of "the Leg Thing" has a peculiar effect on people. Because they can actually see it, it is usually remembered more than any other one. And because it is simple to do, you will probably see more of these kinds of healing than anything else you do.

(Frances)

Two Healings at One Time

One night a man who had been in an accident about thirty-seven years prior came for healing. His back had been severely injured. Someone who was with him suggested that he also have his ear prayed for because he was completely deaf in that ear. Charles asked him what caused the deafness. He replied that it happened the same time his back was injured.

Normally Charles would have put his fingers in the person's ears and commanded the deaf spirit to come out, or commanded the "hair-like" nerves in the ears to come alive. But before he could do that, God clearly spoke to him and said, "Grow out his leg, and he will hear!" Who ever heard of growing out a leg to heal a deaf ear?

We certainly had not, but Charles was obedient.

He said, "Sit down. God said to grow your leg out, and you will be able to hear." I'm glad the man didn't have time to think that over because he might have thought Charles was crazy. Charles measured his legs, and one was about three inches shorter than the other. He commanded the back to be healed. Then he commanded his muscles, nerves, ligaments and tendons to be adjusted and his leg to grow.

The leg grew quickly to full length, and Charles tested his ear. He could hear perfectly! He went all over the church telling everyone that he could hear with his deaf ear. He was so excited about hearing that he forgot to check his back for about an hour. Then he discovered his back was healed, too. Apparently the injury had pinched or damaged a nerve to his ear and caused nerve deafness. This was a new insight for us into God's healing world.

Hundreds have been healed this same way since we discovered there is obviously a connection between nerve deafness and back problems. When the tiny, hair-like nerves inside the ear have died because of a disease or high fever, we have learned to command a creative miracle of life to the nerves.

Because growing out arms and legs seems so commonplace, we overlooked the vast field of miracles that belongs in this type of healing. God has since revealed more and more miracles relating to back, muscle and nerve adjustments.

People who have had chronic back problems for, say, thirty years have been healed simply by commanding the vertebrae and discs to line up and be healed. So try it on everyone you know – you can't hurt them. We always say, "When in doubt, grow it out!"

On a recent trip to a foreign country, a person in a wheelchair had a broken spine. I grew the man's legs out, commanded a new spine in his body, and in less than thirty minutes we saw him walking across the stage, pushing his wife in the wheelchair he had been in for twenty years.

Drug Addiction

A man named Al came to one of our services recently and told us an unusual story. Around midnight he was sound asleep in a motel room. The manager, thinking the room was vacant, entered the room. Al thought he was a burglar, jumped out of bed and, in his hurry, caught his feet in the bedding. He fell against a chest of drawers and hit the wall. This caused some discs and vertebrae to go out of alignment because they were fractured. The doctors said he had multiple fractures. Further, his muscles, nerves, tendons and ligaments were all torn badly.

For six years he had surgery every year, trying to eliminate enough of the pain so that he could bear it. To help the situation, the doctor had prescribed a strong pain killer. Not only did the excruciating pain persist, but the man discovered after a while that he was hooked on the prescribed drugs.

We sat the man on a chair and measured his legs. They were approximately two inches off. Thus, we commanded a creative miracle and the healing of all the vertebrae, discs, muscles, tendons, ligaments and nerves. We also commanded all of the scar tissue to be healed and then rebuked the pain in Jesus' name.

When he got up from the chair after seeing his legs "grow" out, he bent over and moved around vigorously.

Then he asked, "May I run around the church?" He jumped off the stage, ran around the church, jumped back on the stage and then jumped up and down as hard as he could, shouting, "The pain is gone! I've been healed!"

Later that night we were ministering to people individually. Suddenly I saw Al again. God impressed me to go directly to him and pray the following: "Father, in Jesus' name, I command a new blood system, cleansed of all drugs. Thank You, Jesus. We believe it's done!"

We never recommend that people stop taking their medicine without the advice of their physician. But later Al reported to us that he threw all of his medicine away on the way home that night. He said he has never had one withdrawal symptom or been in need of the medicine since. In our communication with Al, we've found out that he has had no back problems. He's also been freed of drug addiction.

Do you see what we learned? A new blood system can correct drug, cigarette or alcohol problems. Now we pray for a new blood system for all addicts so that there will be no craving for the drugs, cigarettes or alcohol.

(Charles)

God is preparing the bride of Christ for His soon-coming return, and He will do it largely through the demonstration of His Spirit and His power. We want you to be a living part of this exciting move of God in these last days. Start growing out arms and legs!

Paul said, *"And my speech and my preaching were not with persuasive words of human wisdom, but in demonstration of the Spirit and of power, that your faith should not be in the wisdom of men but in the power of God"* (I Corinthians 2:4-5). And remember, if Charles and Frances can do it, YOU can do it, too!

(Frances)

Chapter Ten

Electrical Frequencies

Your body is completely made up of cells; blood cells, skin cells, brain cells, etc. and around all of these cells there are electrical frequencies which flow and keep them operating.

We listen and learn all the time from other people; doctors have told us that when the electrical frequencies in a person's body are in harmony and in balance, no disease can live in that body.

This really got our attention! Jesus healed all who came to Him. We personally don't believe He healed all who attended His meetings, because the Sadducees and Pharisees and the ones who tried to kill Him were there. They came to Him physically to scoff but they did not come to Him with any belief but the Bible says that all who came to Him believing were healed (Matthew 4:24). He knew a lot of secrets that we don't know and we have yet to discover.

The statement about disease not being able to live in a perfectly balanced body intrigued us. One of the things that we believe with our heart and soul is that if the doctors can do it with medicine and skills, we can do it with the power of God so we believers become "practicing" evangelists. Doctors are called "practicing" physicians because they constantly practice, so I guess we can do the same thing.

We were in a meeting and a lady came up who stated, "I have an environmental disease. I am in pain twenty-four hours a day and I have lost the sight in one eye. This pain is non-stop because it never ceases." She said that she had formerly been an executive secretary but at this particular point, the function of her mind had so deteriorated from this environmental disease that she had difficulty addressing twelve Christmas cards that year.

We thought this was an excellent thing to try out on her because you cannot lose whenever you lay hands on somebody. We said, "In the name of Jesus we command the electrical frequencies in every cell in your body to be in harmony and in balance." Doctors tell us that if your body is in harmony and in balance, the good cells digest the sick cells. When it is digested, it doesn't exist anymore, so the good cells eliminate the bad cells and your human body recreates good cells. In chemotherapy which is often used on cancer patients, the chemotherapy destroys or digests the good cells as well as the bad cells but with the electrical frequencies, the good cells are not harmed whatsoever.

After we made this command on this lady, she fell out under the power of God and when she got up she almost screamed because she had no pain left. She was literally jumping with joy and went dancing back to her seat when about three or four minutes later she came screaming up because she said, "I can see, I can see, I can see!" God had instantly healed her eye and taken all the pain out. We asked her to really test this for us and to contact us in two or three weeks.

Where her mind had blanked out and she couldn't even address twelve Christmas cards three weeks previously, she wrote us a four page letter on a computer, absolutely perfect, sentence structure perfect, every word spelled correctly and she told us what the effects of the healing were, that her mind was brought back to normal, her eyesight was normal and there has not been any pain in her body from that day to this!

This is the same command we made on a lady who had Parkinson's disease and we have seen many similar cases healed by this very simple little command.

Recently a man around sixty years of age attended a service, suffering horribly from environmental disease which had plagued him for eighteen years. He said for all of the eighteen years he had had nothing but excruciating, continuous pain in his body. We laid hands on him and made the very simple electrical frequency command and he instantly fell out under the power of God. He was there for quite a long time. When he got up he said, "I have no pain, but I don't want to give a testimony because I took pain medicine before I came."

He came back twenty-four hours later with an awesome testimony of no pain medication of any kind and said he had had absolutely no pain whatsoever in his body for the first time in eighteen years!

We use this particular command on many different diseases. One with which we have been seeing some good results is Chronic Fatigue Syndrome. This is something apparently new which has cropped up in the medical field and yet it seemed like a tremendous number of people have the same comment, "I'm tired all the time. I'm exhausted. I can't seem to get rested." We make exactly the same command for that as we do the environmental disease or multiple sclerosis or muscular dystrophy. Remember that it is not a prayer because Jesus never prayed for the sick. It is a command, so firmly get it fixed in your mind to say, "In the name of Jesus, we command the electrical frequencies in every cell in your body to be in harmony and in balance. Thank you, Jesus."

One of the most important things that we have learned in healing is for people to say, "Thank you," as soon as the prayer or the command is completed. Many times people are so aware of the presence of God as they are being healed that they simply forget to say anything. But encourage people to constantly say, "Thank you, Jesus, thank you, Jesus, thank you, Jesus." When you say that, what you are really saying to God is, "I've got it, I've got it, I've got it!" No one can say those three words too often.

What goes wrong in Parkinson's disease?

The progressive death of nerve cells in the substantia nigra, deep within the brain, leaves the nerve fibers in the movement control centers with too little dopamine, a chemical messenger. Patients develop tremors and rigidity. Why the neurons die isn't known.

There are many commands which we use over and over again on many people and the electrical frequencies is one of them. Two nights in a row men came up to us with Parkinson's Disease who were shaking violently as this often makes you do. They said the doctors had been unable to do anything for it. Frances made the command in both instances and commanded all the electrical frequencies in every cell in the body to be in harmony and in balance and there is nothing more dramatic than to see somebody standing there with a body that is shaking all over and hands that are violently vibrating suddenly stop because the power of God has healed them but that's exactly what happened.

A young man brought his mother to one of our services because she was suffering from severe headaches. The pain in her head was so severe that they shaved her head two and three times a week. Whether it was the growing or the weight of the hair we do not know, but Frances laid hands on her and not knowing what else to do, she said, "In the name of Jesus, I command all of the electrical frequencies in every cell in your body to be in harmony and in balance." Frances laid hands on her and while she was going down under the power, she screamed, "I'm healed! No more pain!" It was an awesome and instant miracle. When she got up off of the floor, she could not believe what had happened to her in the twinkling of an eye and that's all it takes with the power of God.

One of the most dramatic healings that we have ever seen occurred during a Saturday morning teaching session. Charles was ministering healing and Frances was sitting on the stage when the pastor came up and whispered, "There's a girl here today who was accidently hit on the head with a large block of wood three years ago which has destroyed her equilibrium and she has difficulty standing, walking or doing anything." He said she had been in constant pain for three years and had been to every doctor, every chiropractor, and every clinic in the area but they all told her exactly the same thing, that there was absolutely nothing that could be done for her.

She suffered pain 24 hours a day and was actually

unable to do anything. She was one of the dancers in the ballet group in the church but she had been unable to dance for three years.

There are times when you need to do more than one thing, so in her case the Holy Spirit spoke and told us to do two things. The first thing we did was to command the electrical frequencies in every cell in her body to be in harmony and in balance and then we did the "NUCCA" on her. She was instantly, totally healed by the power of God. She stood there in the most beautiful simple way and looked up and said, "I'm healed. I don't have any-more pain."

Frances said, "If you are healed, then you will be able to dance." The musicians came up and this woman who had been unable to do anything or even walk straight for three years did the most beautiful ballet dance any-one could have ever seen. This was in her home church and the church knew what her condition was and the electricity of the Holy Spirit burst so upon the entire au-dience that they gave her an instant standing ovation and every person in the house burst into tears. Thank you, Jesus for that wonderful healing power.

Chapter Eleven

Carpal Tunnel Syndrome

Ministering healing is a constantly changing and improving opportunity. The more we minister healing, the more new ways we learn. We listen to medical doctors and chiropractors and have discovered innumerable successful ways to help people because new diseases and new "cures" crop up all the time. We often wonder if it is because people are living longer, which they are, or is it that we have gone into more complicated jobs. Carpal tunnel syndrome is not one which is relegated to old age because it normally affects younger people, especially people who are computer operators, butchers, carpenters, hairdressers, or who work at any kind of a job which requires a tremendous amount of action in the wrist area.

Many times operators in these various jobs hold their hands or their fingers in the wrong position. Many computer operators hold their wrists down and their hands up and this often causes inflammation and swelling in that part of the wrist. Many of the flight attendants on airplanes who push carts or who do heavy work and heavy lifting with their wrists discover that they have what the medical world calls Carpal Tunnel Syndrome.

Recently a chiropractor told us about the common problem today among people who use their wrists a lot.

It can cause such pain in the hand and wrist area that some individuals are unable to sleep or perform their work.

In the hinge of the wrist there exists a "tunnel" which houses ligaments and tendons. When the tunnel becomes inflamed or swollen through misuse or excessive use of the wrist, the passage is closed to varying degrees. Pain, weakness or other discomforts in the wrist area arise. The ligaments or tendons may be stretched or jammed.

To heal carpal tunnel syndrome, place your thumb on one side of the soft spot in the wrist joint and a finger on the opposite side. Command the tunnel to open, both the inflammation and the swelling to be healed, and the tendons and ligaments to go back to normal length, position, and strength. Command them to be healed in the name of Jesus.

There is an extremely simple way to test for carpal tunnel syndrome. Have the person put his or her thumb and little finger together to form an "o." Then put your forefinger in the circle and pull through the "o." If the person has carpal tunnel syndrome, you can pull your finger through easily. Once it is healed, you won't be able to pull through the thumb and little finger.

Miracles for carpal tunnel syndrome happen regularly. Recently Frances had her hair done at a beauty parlor in preparation for having our pictures taken.

Her hair stylist worked carefully, feverishly and patiently to accomplish a perfect hairdo.

I noticed she wore a steel brace on her left wrist, extending about eight inches up her arm. When I asked her if she had carpal tunnel syndrome, she answered, "Yes." She added that she had taken care of sixty-two wigs that day.

Because of the strain this had put on her left hand, she could hardly move her wrist.

I asked her if she would like for God to heal it. The minute she got a break I did what we had learned and gave the commands. We had tested the woman's strength, and there was no resistance when I moved my finger through the loop she had made by holding her thumb and little finger in position. After we gave the commands, we immediately tested her strength again.

She was utterly amazed! She shook her wrist and in a few minutes had removed the brace. She was working free of pain. When we talked to her about two weeks later, she was exuberant with praise to God for completing this much-needed miracle.

A medical doctor recently called Frances to tell her his excitement about divine healing success after he watched our fifteen-hour video series and read the book How to Heal the Sick. She told him about carpal tunnel syndrome healings, explained to him how to test this before and after ministering, and how to do it.

About two weeks later this same physician called her again, but with even more excitement. He said many patients with carpal tunnel syndrome had come to him.

Every single one was healed when he did what God had shown us. Then he asked with a laugh, "What should I do with the thousands of fliers I bought, telling how surgery could help heal the problem?"

What about feet?

A corresponding soft spot is located in the ankle area. Just in the bend of your ankle, beneath your ankle bone, you can have the same condition. This is called

Tarsal Tunnel Syndrome. This is healed exactly the same way as the wrist although not nearly as many people have this problem as have carpal tunnel syndrome.

The Tarsal Tunnel

The tarsal tunnel contains the posterior tibial nerve and several blood vessels and tendons. It begins behind and above the ankle, moving around the inside of the ankle and into the bottom of the foot. If the nerve is damaged or compressed by trauma, swelling or growths surrounding tendons, blood vessels or bones, a painful condition called "tarsal tunnel syndrome" can result.

Each foot has 26 bones. This means that you have a great opportunity for a lot of those to get out of adjustment or out of place or turned because you're wearing the wrong shoes or maybe you have a weak ankle. You command the tunnel to open up and all the ligaments to be made whole in the name of Jesus.

On this one you could add, "In the name of Jesus, I command every bone in both feet to go into place and stay there in Jesus' name."

Another ailment, tendonitis or "tennis elbow," is healed by the carpal tunnel "thing." If you will be alert to the nudgings of the Holy Spirit, you will discover many new ways to see someone healed.

You can even do it to yourself and always remember, "If Charles and Frances can do it, YOU can do it, too!"

Chapter Twelve
A "Stay-At-Home" Goes Out!

Norma Stibbs went on a trip to the Philippines with us some 20 years ago. She stayed in the background all the time but saw incredible healings, including blind eyes opened. She has been on many overseas trips since then and she has been consistent in her tremendous faith and love of God at all times! We have watched her grow tremendously in the Lord ever since. She and her husband, John, now pastor a church. You'll find her story fascinating.

All of my life I had an overwhelming desire to see people healed, but I never dreamed that God could ever use me in such a wonderful way. I was a housewife who stayed home and took care of my family and home. I enjoyed what I did but there was a longing on the inside of me for something more.

When I heard about Charles and Frances Hunter and the ministry they have I knew I had to know more. I asked my church to order their video healing school and I agreed to be in charge of it and to conduct a class every Saturday morning. I had no idea what was about to happen to me! As the classes began I knew something different was taking place in me.

Charles and Frances made healing look so simple and easy but always let you know that it was in the name of Jesus and by the power of God's Holy Spirit. The method of healing with the arms and legs growing out was so incredible because you could see it happen. I watched the other people in the class and saw the excitement in them as they watched the videos. After the class we did exactly what they said and found those who had back pain, neck pain, etc. As we began to minister to these people you could hear the snappings and crackling of bones as they were being healed. We had slipped discs, degenerated discs, bursitis, arthritis and stiff necks which were instantly healed. I knew everything that was happening was by the Holy Spirit but it was happening through me.

The words which kept coming to me that forever changed my life were "If Charles and Frances can do it, you can do it too." God is no respecter of persons. If they could do it, I could too. I stepped out in the most incredible faith and simply believed those words.

I started laying hands on the sick believing they would be healed. God works through faith. I have seen tumors dissolve right in front of my eyes as I curse them in the name of Jesus. I started commanding deaf ears to open and they pop open. I went into the hospital to visit a woman who was in traction because of back injuries, I asked her if she had to stay in traction all the time and she replied it was just six hours a day. I asked if I could check to see if her legs were the same length, and her one leg was a good two inches shorter. I said, "Watch what God is about to do." I made the commands and her leg grew out and she got up, moved around and was healed. Her back problems were instantly healed and the next day after her doctor checked her out she was discharged from the hospital.

Since then I have traveled to many nations with Charles and Frances. On a trip to Honduras, Frances asked me to go to the wheelchair section. At that moment all the faith that I had felt like it drained out my toes. What was I going to do if they didn't get healed. Then I remembered what was taught on the videos, you make the command in the name of Jesus and go on. It's up to God to heal them. The minute Frances said to start ministering I went to the first wheelchair and said, "Silver and gold have I none, but such as I have I give to you, in the name of Jesus rise up and walk." Nothing happened. I went to the next wheelchair and said the same thing, nothing happened. Then I remembered if Charles and Frances can do it, I can do it too. My faith was coming back. I went to the third wheelchair and as I began to say the same thing again, I heard everyone shouting and turned to see the man in the first wheelchair stand up and walk. I turned back to minister to the woman in the third wheelchair and before I could finish she got up. I was so excited I went like fire and just said, "In the name of Jesus rise up and walk," and six people came out of wheelchairs!

Needless to say my life has never been the same. It's so wonderful to see the Holy Spirit heal through you. I've thought about all the healings that have taken place since I first watched the videos and all the lives that have been changed and I guess the one that stands out in my mind the most was a man in his late 50's who was blind since birth and wanted so badly to see. I laid my thumbs on his eyes and made the commands and rebuked the spirit of blindness. I removed my thumbs and he still couldn't see. I said the same thing again and when I removed my thumbs he said he could see light. That wasn't good enough, so I began to make the same command again, but he spoke out and said, "I want to see her (meaning me)." Through my tears I lifted my voice to the Lord and said, "God give him the desire of his heart, open his eyes and let him see me." I removed my thumbs and he opened his eyes and saw me perfectly. I was the very first person he had ever seen in his lifetime. We hugged and praised God together and everyone was shouting. I asked how many of them wanted to receive Jesus and their hands shot up in the air. They prayed and received Jesus and then received the baptism of the Holy Spirit.

I've learned that healing is the easiest way to bring people to the Lord. I've shown the video healing course about 30 times. I've purchased them and placed them in churches where I've ministered and also sent them to Ireland and Ivory Coast, Africa. I've been blessed to train thousands how to heal the sick as I've traveled to 23 nations and throughout the United States.

I now have my own church and the first thing we did was to show the video healing school and train the people to minister to the sick. Charles and Frances gave me the confidence that changed my life, and "if I can do it, you can do it, too." Get ready for a life changing experience!

(Norma Stibbs)

Chapter Thirteen

Migraine Headaches and Tic Douloureux
(Trigeminal Neuralgia)

Recently we visited with Hilton Sutton, president of Mission to America and a great Bible prophecy teacher. He shared with us for the first time that he had a problem called tic douloureux, or trigeminal neuralgia. We had seen only a few people healed of this painful affliction and did not know of any medical procedure that would help the problem.

The American Medical Association Family Medical Guide, published by Random House (New York, 1991), describes this affliction as pain from a damaged nerve.

This kind of neuralgia rarely affects anyone under fifty except in cases of multiple sclerosis. The trigeminal nerve is a major nerve in the face. If it is damaged, the result is severe pain that is usually felt on only one side of the face. Although it is not life-threatening, trigeminal neuralgia can be distressing and disabling.

We have talked to people who say it is one of the most painful afflictions there is. In fact, it is sometimes called the suicide disease. This same medical guide reports that the pain of trigeminal neuralgia shoots through one side of the face along the length of the nerve. It may last for a few seconds or as long as a minute or more. While it lasts it can be excruciating.

Sometimes attacks occur every few minutes for several days or weeks for no apparent reason. They may then fade, but stabbing pains usually return with decreasing intervals between them. Attacks may eventually become almost continuous. In some cases occasional muscular spasms accompany the pain and cause a facial tic (twitching) or paralysis.

Hilton told us that for eight long and painful years he had suffered with tic douloureux. It was getting so bad that he was considering canceling some of his speaking engagements. Then he said, "The medical world has discovered a surgery that can stop this excruciating pain." We listened intently, because when a cause and a cure are discovered, we often find clues to a healing that God has in store for us.

He explained the type of surgery performed. They drill a hole through the skull into a place where a blood vessel or artery is too close to a nerve. Then they place a medical wedge between the two, which stops the pain.

Our response was "Thank You, Jesus!" Immediately we laid hands on Hilton's head and commanded a divine wedge to separate the vessel or artery and the nerve. We gave thanks to Jesus. When Hilton called a month later, he said the only pain he had experienced since that day was a headache resulting from a stressful situation.

Another month went by, and we talked again on the day we were writing this story. Hilton said he has had no more pain. Glory to God for healing him!

And thank You, Jesus, for showing us how to heal tic douloureux.

However, Hilton Sutton was so far behind on his work and his speaking engagements because of the excruciating pain of tic douloureux, when God healed him, he immediately started rebooking and overbooked himself including a long trip to Singapore and Malaysia. When he came back he was in the same condition he was in before God healed him. Hilton went to the hospital and had the operation done. The doctors worked for about four hours and said they'd never seen so many tangled nerves and blood vessels in their entire lives.

Hilton called us and said, "I know I was healed by God but I brought it back on myself through overwork and through stress."

Stress is one of the worst things in the world to which any of us can subject ourselves because it brings on innumerable diseases. Hilton still maintains to this day that God healed him but he lost it through carelessness on his part.

The Bible says, *"Cast all your cares on Him, and He will give you rest!"*

Chapter Fourteen

The "NUCCA"

We learn new things all the time which really excite us. We believe if doctors and chiropractors can do it, we can do it with the power of God.

Following is an article which appeared in a magazine recently which has really taught us a lot about doing what we call "The NUCCA Thing."

IS YOUR HEAD ON STRAIGHT

By Glenn Cripe, D.C.

Just when you thought you have tried everything, have you checked to see if your head is on straight?

Most people have experienced back pain or spinal-related problems sometime in their life. There are numerous approaches to achieving relief from this often times disabling pain. There are procedures that vary as widely as bed rest to medications, acupuncture, acupressure, and then the extreme: surgery. All of these and other systems have had their degrees of successes and failures. Perhaps the one thing that can be said for certain is that there is no cure-all, no one hundred percent solution for all back problems. It is after all, a very complicated problem. The spinal column, various layers of muscles and the nervous system largely make up the structure that not only allows us to remain upright under gravity, but also allows us to bend, twist and tilt.

In seeking out help, most people will use the more conservative approaches first, like bed rest, and then keep moving toward the more extreme, like surgery, if they have not obtained the relief they need.

In this arena of back pain procedures, there is a system that offers still another approach. It's conservative, cost efficient, but, more importantly, extremely precise and painless. This procedure is named NUCCA after the National Upper Cervical Chiropractic Association. The NUCCA principles were developed in Michigan by Drs. Ralph Gregory and John Grostic in the 1940s. NUCCA was formed in 1965 as a national organization recognized by the federal government. NUCCA is a specialty within the chiropractic profession that concentrates specifically on returning the head and neck to normal.

Most conditions that can benefit from chiropractic care usually begin and can end in the neck. Falls, a whiplash type of accident, or a twist of the neck can all result in the relationship of the head and neck going off center. By adjusting the head and neck, the entire spine, including the pelvis, can return back toward normal. This must be done before spinal balance can be attained.

The pelvis is the foundation for the spine; hence it supports the spine. As the head shifts off center, the pelvis must also shift. This is to keep the body as upright as possible. If the head is in its normal position, the pelvis will be directly under it. But if the head and neck misalign, the muscles of the back will automatically tighten to shift the pelvis so it will be as directly under the head as pos-

sible. This shifting of the structure of spine and pelvis can be the cause of many back problems, such as low back spasms, headaches, poor posture, or tingling pain in the extremities etc. Unless the head and neck are returned back to their normal position, you may never really have a long term correction with long term results.

Because the pelvis is the supporting structure of the spine, NUCCA, through precise instrumentation, measures its displacement and uses it as a guage in determining if the patient is in adjustment. Three very exacting x-rays are taken and analyzed before any type of treatment is rendered. Each person has his or her unique type of misalignment pattern which must be precisely determined. Once the type and degree of misalignment have been established, the doctor is able to direct a slight and controlled pressure into the neck at a particular spot, which will then bring the head and neck back towards normal. The closer the doctor can restore the head and neck to normal, the more stable and long lasting the adjustment will be. As the body returns to normal the muscles will pull evenly, relieving muscle spasms. Swelling around the nerves can subside, relieving the pinched nerve feeling. Postural changes can occur along with the removal of stress on the weight-bearing joints (hips, low back).

After the correction has taken place, both the doctor and patient should see significant results in postural changes. Within a three to six week period, symptomatic relief should occur.

Each case is unique but generally symptoms can begin to alter from as soon as a few hours up to four to six weeks from the adjustment. After all, it usually has

*taken time to get out of shape. It will also take time for
the tissue and nerves to heal.*

*As an alternative to correcting back problems,
NUCCA has had wonderful results and research docu-
mented over the past 45 years. So when you get to the
point where you thought you've tried everything, you may
want to find out if your head is on straight.*

Dr. Glenn Cripe of Newport Beach is a Doctor of Chiropractics specializing in NUCCA.

The daughter of a friend of ours had twin babies a
couple of years ago and from the time of the delivery she
had never been able to do any of her housework or the
normal tasks associated with being a wife and a mother.
She had been to many doctors and chiropractors and had
received no relief whatsoever until she found out about
this NUCCA treatment. She went and had three treat-
ments. After the third treatment, she was able to do normal housework and she has remained healed ever since.

We believe whatever can be done by a doctor or
chiropractor can be done by using the power of God!

The first time we ever tried this was when a young
man who had been in an automobile accident and was in
excruciating pain in his back came to one of our services. We sat him down and measured his legs as we do
when we do "The Leg Thing." He had one leg over four
inches shorter than the other from this accident to his
back. We did not do the usual "Leg Thing" but instead
we laid our finger along his jawbone and made the command for the NUCCA. We said, "In the name of Jesus,
we command the brain stem to be centered over the spine
to relieve all problems in the back and we command the
brain stem and the head to line up perfectly with the
spinal column. After we had made this simple command

in Jesus' name, we sat him down, his leg had grown out to absolute normal length with the other one and he had no pain whatsoever! He spent the rest of the night rejoicing and praising God. What a thrill to see this work the first time we tried it.

We have done this many times since then with remarkable success.

If you will look at the diagrams you will see what happens before and after an accident and it doesn't have to be an automobile accident. It can be any kind where we stretch our body abnormally but which needs to be taken care of.

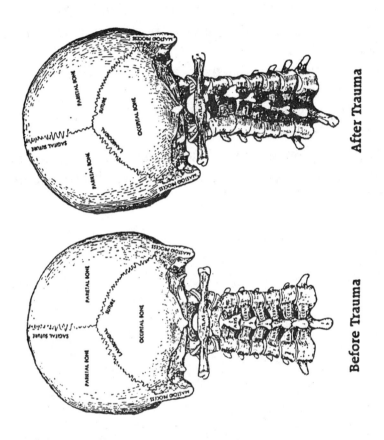

After Trauma

Before Trauma

Here's what happens before trauma and after trauma: Prior to a spinal trauma, the 12 lb. head is evenly centered over the neck. Post trauma, the head has shifted away from center. To compensate, the neck buckles from its intended position putting undue stress on muscles and ligaments.

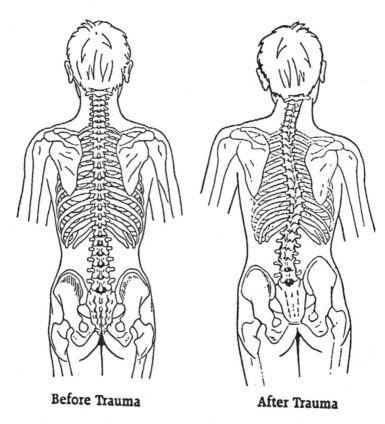

Before Trauma   After Trauma

The spinal column remains straight and balanced as long as the head is centered over the neck. Following an accident, the head has shifted away from center. To compensate for the change and to keep the body in balance, the entire spinal column begins to buckle. Over time, an injury to the head and neck can cause low back pain.

Chapter Fifteen

The Difference Between A Miracle & A Healing

We all wish that we could lay hands on the sick and see them instantly recover. We love it when we lay hands on a person who has palsy, make a command in the name of Jesus, and then see them stop shaking immediately. This awesome miracle recently happened to us.

A lady got in the wrong line and Charles laid hands on her for diabetes and when she fell under the power I said, "Charles, no, that's not diabetes, that's Parkinson's Disease." So while she was on the floor, we made the electrical frequency command which you learned about in this book and she looked right up at us and she said, "I'm healed because I stopped shaking!" She got up off of the floor, held her arms up in the air and where she had been violently shaking before, there was not even a slight tremor!

This brought the whole audience to their feet in a standing ovation to Jesus because it was the first healing of the evening and so it was a real, real special time! How we wish they could all be like this!

A lady came to a recent meeting of ours who said she had been in an automobile accident 36 years before. For all those years she had suffered excruciating pain day and night with no relief. She said she had slept very little in the 36 years because the pain was so intense. She had been to doctors, she had been to chiropractors, she had been to every source you could think of, and she said, "I have not lived in 36 years. I have just existed." Her face showed the pain she had been through.

A simple command was made, and how we wish there had been a camera to catch the expression on her face! She was totally shocked to discover that "suddenly" (and that's how quickly it happened!) the pain disappeared 100%. She bent over, she ran, she walked up and down stairs, she did everything you could think of and there was not one sign of pain left in her body!

These are the kinds of healings we wish happened all the time but don't get discouraged when they don't, but be excited when they do.

A little boy came to our service with rheumatoid arthritis. He was nine years old, and his parents told us he had never had a day without pain. This is really difficult on a child because it made it impossible for him to play or participate in any games with other children, but their great faith brought him hundreds of miles to come to the service. His healing was quick because children are easily healed since their faith is so simple. We made the usual command for rheumatoid arthritis and suddenly he looked up with simple childlike faith and said, "Do you know I don't have any pain in my body at all?"

He immediately began feeling his knees and feeling his feet and feeling his hands and he looked at me and said, "I don't have anything. I don't have a bit of pain anywhere!" Then he took off and ran down the aisle of the church to tell his mother that the pain was all gone.

This is the kind that, of course, excites the person

prayed for, the person who did the praying, and an entire congregation! How we wish all healings would be that way and we believe some day they will! The instant one is the miracle healing!

But there is another wonderful kind of a healing that takes place over time. Many people when they come forward are praying and hoping and expecting their healing to be an instant healing, but what happens if they don't get healed immediately?

Don't let the devil steal your healing from you! The power of God has gone into the person prayed for and the power of God will continue to work in you! Many people, if they do not get an instant healing, make the mistake of going back to their seat and saying immediately, "I didn't get my healing." This is allowing the devil to steal what happened to you, so don't ever listen when the devil tells that to you. When we're laying hands on the sick we need to encourage people to continue to believe for their healing.

There has been a lot of comment both pro and con by the Word Faith movement which taught that all you have to say is, "By His stripes I am healed," and you will be healed. This has worked for many people and we don't want to discourage you from standing on the Word of God. Our pastor, John Osteen, taught his congregation an incredible truth which we think helps a lot in this situation.

In Romans 4:17 it says that we can call into being those things which be not as though they were, but Pastor John said, "You cannot call the things which **are** as though they are **not.**" In other words, if you have cancer, you cannot stand up and say, "I do not have cancer in my body." The provision for your healing is there, but you are not healed until you are healed. You cannot deny that you have cancer.

We have heard many people say, "I'm not going to go to the doctor because by His stripes I am healed." One case that particularly stands out in my mind of someone calling something that was as though it were not was a woman who had a huge breast cancer. I asked her if I could lay hands on her and she said, "What for?"

I said, "I heard you had cancer."

She said, "I absolutely do not. I am healed."

I could see the size of this cancer which was about the size of a grapefruit. It was still there and although the provision was there for her healing, she had not been healed yet. She died.

One of the things that we want to encourage you to do is always pray first. If when you pray you do not get healed, and you pray again and again, then there is a time to go to the doctor. Charles and I have never hesitated to go to a doctor. All of the incredible healings that I have had have been because I went to a doctor and found out what the problem was, came home and told Charles. He prayed for me and I got healed because sometimes we can pray amiss or we can command amiss.

At this point, we really want to share something right from our hearts. Once in a while you will pray and you don't get healed and the condition worsens and worsens until something has to be done. Don't get upset.

Several years ago I had to have an artificial knee replacement in my right leg. I believed up to the very last minute that God was going to give me a new kneecap and even insisted before I went to surgery that the doctor take a last minute X-ray, but God did not put in a new one.

Now what do I do? I had believed for my healing, but I didn't get it. I have more new parts than I have original parts but the knee was not one of them. I didn't intend to hobble around crippled the rest of my life so I just said, "Thank you, Jesus," and we asked God to guide the surgeon's hand but I did not say, "I have received a new knee." I suppose I could have said that because up until that time I had been walking bone on bone and it really hurt but when I had the knee replacement put in, the pain totally disappeared. I did have a new knee but not the kind I had expected.

Well, Frances, aren't you ashamed to tell people that you had to have a knee replacement? No! God can take any mess and make a miracle out of it. The doctor who did the surgery accepted Jesus as His Savior and Lord; we ministered healing all throughout the hospital as people came into my room when they heard I was there and we have our video tapes on HOW TO HEAL THE SICK in the doctor's waiting room. Hallelujah!

So you see, if you have to submit to an operation, get healed one way or another. You might say, "Well, didn't you fail to get healed because you lacked faith?"

I don't know. Ask God. I don't understand why I didn't get a new knee, I don't understand why I did get a new heart supernaturally.

Let me explain healing in this way. Most of us have a thermostat in our house for various reasons. Sometimes we need our house cooler and sometimes we need it a little warmer. When we went to Russia it was a real cold day and I said, "How do you get the room warm?"

They said, "Close the windows."

That was a shock to me so I said, "Well, how do you get it cool in the summertime?"

They said, "Open the windows."

They don't have thermostats over there but most of us do.

Pastor Osteen, in the same sermon, said that when you come in from the cold and maybe it's snowing outside and maybe your thermostat is set at 60 degrees and it's as cold as can be. What is the first thing you do? You go to the thermostat and turn it up. Now, what is the second thing you do? If it doesn't immediately jump to 72 degrees, do you kick the thermostat and say, "Well, it doesn't work, I'll just break that thing because it doesn't work?"

No, that's not what you do at all. You are perfectly content to wait until the temperature goes up and we all know it takes a little time to get a thermostat from 60 up to 72, so all we do is patiently wait.

The same thing is true of healings. Sometimes you get an instant healing but sometimes you have to wait. Sometimes healings can take place over a 24-hour period. Sometimes it might even take a month or two before the healing is complete but we always recommend to people that you keep thanking Jesus for the healing while it is going on. Don't let the devil come in and rob you with doubt and unbelief about your healing but keep thanking God and saying, "Thank you, Jesus, I know my healing is on the way."

If I were you, right now I would set my thermostat at 72 for whatever is wrong with your body. If you're down to 50 or 40 degrees it might take you a little while to get up to 72 but remember that you are on the way.

The testimony of Gene Lilly is a perfect example of what if you don't see your healing instantly.

He did not believe in healing because he had never been in any church where they taught healing but God directed him and his family to move to Orlando, Florida. When he got there he went to a large Full Gospel church and he couldn't believe what he saw because people were clapping their hands, praising the Lord, and singing. Something began to happen on the inside of him. Then the pastor made a statement, "If you're sick, the Lord will heal you. If you're broke, the Lord wants to prosper you. If you're lost, He wants to save you."

Suddenly Gene Lilly became aware of the fact that God was still alive today and that He could heal him.

He had been sick for 19 years with an extreme case of multiple sclerosis. He had scar tissue on the brain, diabetes, high cholesterol, high triglycerides and the doctors had told him that he was dying.

He said, "Someone gave me a copy of the book, SINCE JESUS PASSED BY by Charles and Frances Hunter. I read it and it really ministered to me. I thought, 'Well, if the Hunters would pray for me because they've had a lot of great healings in their ministry (not because of the fact that they had healing power in them, but because of the fact that Charles and Frances had seen people healed) they would have the faith I was looking for. It would be easy for them to believe and pray the prayer of faith.'

"I found out that they were coming to Orlando. I knew that was my night to be healed!

"There were no steps in the building where I was

going to be healed, so I didn't even take my walker!

"Phyllis and Doug helped me out of the car and half dragged, half carried me into the building. The Holy Spirit had revealed to me that when I went to be prayed for, it would be no different than when I prayed the sinner's prayer – I would be made whole! I had no doubt about it! There was no reason to think the Bible was not right; it was right and meant what it said!

"People were getting healed all over the place. A man just four or five seats from me was healed of a deaf ear.

"Praise God!

"A lot of people I knew got healed, and I thought, 'Hallelujah! this is my night!'

"We stood up then and started singing and praising the Lord. When I stood I got such a severe pain in my back I didn't think I was going to be able to sit down. Here came the word from the devil. He said, 'You're going to have to leave because you can't sit down.' I just believed God and said, 'God, you wouldn't want me out of here; even if I wasn't going to be healed, Lord, you wouldn't want me to leave here. This is too beautiful.'

"I did sit down, and as soon as I started to sit the pain left.

"I wondered when it would happen to me. The service continued and nothing happened to me. The service ended – and still I wasn't healed.

"But I knew this was my night to be healed.

"Could I have been wrong? 'But Jesus, it is in your Word and I believe it.' They dismissed the service. Then Frances said, 'If anybody has come with a need that hasn't been met, we want you to come forward. We're going to pray for you.'

"When Frances said that I got up out of my chair and started making my way to the front, one row at a time, hanging onto the chairs because I didn't have my walker and nobody was taking me up. I finally got up there. Frances said to me, 'What's your problem?'

"'I've got multiple sclerosis, scar tissue on my brain, sugar diabetes, high cholesterol and I'm dying.'

"At that point I got the biggest surprise of my life. She looked at me and said, 'Praise Jesus!'

"I thought she had to be the most hard-hearted woman in the world to say something like that to somebody dying, but then I looked into her eyes, and for the first time in my life I saw somebody who believed that I could be healed. She very simply, excitedly, said, 'What you need is a Jesus overhaul.' She placed both of her hands gently on the sides of my head and said, 'Jesus, overhaul him!'

"My faith ignited – she didn't limit God!

"She didn't ask God to keep me from hurting. She didn't say, 'If it be thy will.' She didn't limit God at all! She said, 'Jesus, overhaul him!'

"She was the first person, I believe, who ever prayed for me who didn't limit God!

"I began falling backwards. I hit the floor like a ton of bricks. I fell under the power of God. I didn't know that would ever happen to me, but it certainly did.

"As I lay there on the floor I remember hitting someone behind me and he went 'oof' and I hit the floor. I later discovered it was the usher catching me. I had gone backwards harder than he expected.

"I knew I had been touched by the power of God.

"As I lay there on the floor it was like there was a great blinding light came before me. It felt like God had a blow torch on the scar tissue on my brain at the back of my head and it was burning. There were waves of light that went over me. Then it was like my spinal cord was a piece of rubber and someone took it and shook it and flopped it around. I don't know how long I was under the power, maybe five or ten minutes or more. I started feeling healing.

"The first thing I noticed was that my feet began to hurt! My feet had been numb for years and I couldn't tell whether my shoes fit or not, but suddenly my shoes began to pinch my feet! I knew something was happening because there had been absolutely no feeling there for years. Praise God, they were actually hurting!

"Then feeling began to come into my legs! Then in my arms!! I started rubbing my arm. I could feel my hand on my arm as I lay there under the power of God. I was not unconscious – I was aware of what was going on and I knew a lot was going on!

"The next thing that happened was, to me, the most exciting part of the miracle God was performing.

"I got up by myself!

"The most difficult thing for an M.S. victim to do is to get up once you are down. Your equilibrium has been lost. It's almost like you're drunk.

"There had to be a great healing!

"I got up!

"I could get up unassisted!

"I knew I had been healed!"

While Gene Lilly felt healing in his body, the results were not visible to anyone else. He crawled and/or hung on to the chairs to get back to his seat and I said, "I'm not moved by what I see, hear, feel, taste, touch or smell, I am moved by what the Word of God says. The Word of God says when we lay hands upon the sick they shall recover and I believe it! He may not look like it, but the healing power of God is working in him."

It was not until 24 hours later that his walking improved but it took five weeks of battling the devil before he was healed!

Gene Lilly's Answer to "What Follows Healing?"

One of the questions most often asked about healings is, "Do they last?"

The same question can be asked about salvation, "Does it last?"

The same answer can be given to both questions, "Not if Satan can prevent it."

But God's Word is true and Jesus made full and complete arrangements while he was visiting earth for our eternal salvation and health.

On Thursday night, December 13, 1973, I was healed of multiple sclerosis, sugar diabetes, scar tissue on my brain, and excessively high cholesterol and triglycerides.

I woke up the next morning, December 14, 1973, with a new experience! I got up feeling good. Glory to God! I cannot remember during nineteen years of sickness, getting up feeling good. I got up whole. I never knew what it was like to feel whole. I had a little spot of pain in my back, but it was like a sore muscle, nothing serious. The whole weekend was real good and so was Monday.

I wanted to get in touch with the doctor. I wanted to find out about my sugar, but he was out of town. Charles and Frances had said during the miracle service that if anyone healed was under the care of a physician or on medication prescribed, to continue the medication until the doctor examined you and let him tell you what to do.

To those who are not familiar with sugar diabetes (Diabetes Mellitus) let me explain a little about it in language I understand. When you have diabetes, the sugar content gets too high in your blood.

In my case, the highest measurement was 639 when it should have been between 80 and 120. This was a severe case of diabetes. The symptoms and reactions I had were weakness and nausea and I would perspire heavily. At times I would pass out (faint). My doctor had me wear a metal bracelet, on the back of which was engraved "diabetic." This was worn so that if I was found unconscious or helpless, I would be properly treated for diabetes. Time (in receiving treatment) is important when this condition exists. I cut the bracelet off the night I was healed!

Diabetics are generally taught how to test the sugar content of the blood so they can regulate the intake of sugar into their blood. A little test tape is inserted into a urine sample and the tape changes color, thus identifying excess sugar. Insulin is the medication normally used to cause the excess sugar to be stored in such places as the liver and muscles; then the sugar is returned to the blood in small quantities. Proper dieting, rest and other care is needed for survival. Too little sugar can cause serious reactions just as well as too much, so you have to maintain a proper balance. I was instructed to drink orange juice and eat candy or other sweets to raise the sugar, and to take insulin along with a restricted diet to lower the sugar content.

When I was not able to reach my doctor the morning after I was healed, to have him examine me, I did what Charles and Frances suggested. I took a pretty large dose of insulin. In about two hours I started getting shaky and weak. I knew this meant I had too little sugar. It meant something had happened! It meant my sugar diabetes had been healed. It was gone! I was excited because this was the first identifiable evidence I had seen of this part of my healing. My faith ignited again! To counteract the effect of the insulin, I started drinking orange juice and eating candy bars, and still felt most of the day like I was going into insulin shock because the sugar was gone out of my blood stream. Praise God. It was gone!

When my doctor got back, I told him I had been healed. He wanted to know who healed me, and I said, "Jesus!"

"Jesus who?" he snapped. He assured me that the Lord couldn't do anything for me and that I was just going to die.

That was when a battle began within me. Satan really got in the door by putting doubt in my mind. God had been so complete in teaching me what His Word said about healing. I believed it! Then He healed me and gave me positive evidences of my healings.

I would periodically check my urine and the test would at times be positive, showing it contained sugar. I would rebuke it, speak the Word, and in ten or fifteen minutes test it again and there would be no sugar! It just doesn't work that way. You either have it, or you don't have it!

It was a demonic presence. I never took any medication for any of the illnesses after that one insulin shot the morning after I was healed. It was interesting to me because at the time of each attack, I had a chance either to pray and battle the devil or accept the sickness. *"Submit yourself therefore to God. Resist the devil, and he will flee from you" (James 4:7 KJV).*

I had a choice each time to confess this powerful promise of God – a choice of submitting myself to God and resisting the devil – or of submitting to the devil and his symptoms and resisting God. Praise God, He had made my belief in His Word so solid that Satan could not shake it. That's why Jesus said it was so important to study the Word and hide it in our hearts. An hour or more each day meditating in the Bible and talking to God is more vital than I thought my life-giving insulin was. I could have died without the insulin, but even more real, I could have died without the Word! It kept me alive with each attack!

I was sure of my healings. They were just like the Word said, "But the negative power of Satan is strong and simple, but very deceiving." He put "doubt" into my mind; it became so strong at times that I was tempted to listen to him. I almost believed him! "Almost thou persuadeth me to be sick."

My life had been directed around sickness for nineteen years, and around my infirmities. My mind had been filled with belief in sickness. The devil is not going to let go of his teachings easily. He wants you to believe, knowing that if you believe him you will succeed in accepting his inflicted physical, mental and spiritual sicknesses.

Believe me, Satan is going to always put up a battle when God is doing a work. My life had revolved around something that belonged to the devil, so he wasn't going to let something happen that would give credit to God, if he could prevent it!

But God's army is ready to do battle against Satan if we will believe in God and listen to His voice. God will always win if we will do our part. He even wins by allowing us to go through trials, difficulties and problems. He makes our faith stronger. He never allows these tests to come just to see if we can fail. He wants us to win, because when we do, it's easier to have faith to believe in Him once we have won the battle.

He allowed me to be severely tried, but I learned to distinguish the silent, soft voice of His Holy Spirit from the boisterous, enticing, deceiving voice of Satan. The symptoms of "his" diseases (I used to call them "mine") came back time after time.

I had been asked to give my testimony at church on Wednesday night a week after my healing. Just before I was to speak, I broke out in a heavy sweat exactly like I always did when my sugar was too high. I almost soaked my clothes in the pew. As I sat there, I got so weak I thought I wasn't going to be able to get up. But I rebuked those thoughts and in my mind I kept thinking, "I'm not going to receive this because the Lord healed me, and I know He healed me because the sugar is gone from my bloodstream. The diabetes is gone, and so I'm not going to accept it and I am going to testify to the church of my healing.

As soon as I got up to testify, all of the symptoms left!

I had heard the very apparent voice of Satan say, by the symptoms and accompanying thought of fear, that I wasn't healed. Doubt came because of the symptoms. But the Word of God had taught me that fear, doubt and sickness all come from the devil. I had received the Word of God in my mind and heart and believed what it said. All the healing scriptures were a part of my inner belief and memory. They were my source of stability and I let them become my thoughts at the time of the symptoms.

I had recorded Psalms 118:17 in my mind and it was available to my memory with each attack of the devil, *"I shall not die, but live, and declare the works of the Lord."* I boldly, quickly and frequently declared the healing of the Lord to everyone I could, but perhaps of more importance, I declared it to myself - in my own mind as thoughts.

When I depended on mind control tactics to battle diseases, I declared to a mirror, "I am well, I am well, I am well." But I didn't declare the works of the Lord. I was now able to testify boldly that it was the Lord who did it. Where I once confessed my infirmities, I now confessed His Word, *"By His stripes, I AM healed."*

I could feel the presence of the Holy Spirit when I was in the church. It was there that God had first removed the symptoms as I stood to declare the works of the Lord. The church daily became my intensive care room and my recovery room during this recovery period. I needed a place sterilized by the cleansing power of the Holy Spirit, to be away from the polluted atmosphere of Satan's deceiving symptoms and lies. Almost every day for the next four or five weeks I went to the church, knelt at the altar alone and talked to God for ten to fifteen minutes. Most of the time, nobody knew this.

You have probably seen a cartoon of a dog chasing a cat as fast as they could run, and suddenly the cat jumped behind a tree and took a deep breath or two, then the chase began again. That's the way I felt. I would go to the church, take a deep breath of the presence of God, and then return home.

I asked others to pray with me when the battle got rough. It got so bad at times after the first week, that I spent the biggest part of that five weeks in the Word, in prayer, and testifying about my healing.

I would, at times, get numbness over my whole body. It would come like waves over my body and then I would rebuke it and say, "I won't receive this; by His stripes I am healed and I know I'm healed. Because I have been healed, I won't accept it back." Right away feeling came back as the numbness left. The numbness would not go immediately, but gradually would go away while I was saying to it, "I won't receive this; by His stripes I am healed!"

There were times when the devil attacked me with this numbness and other symptoms that we met in a full battle in the bathroom. I don't mind telling you I really got to shouting the Word at him a few times because, you know, he has a little problem with his hearing. I know there is nothing in volume. It is the authority of Jesus by which the devil is defeated, but it helps me when I use a little volume!

These symptoms were just as real to me as the actual diseases. I believe I had every symptom of every illness with which I had previously been afflicted. The pain of the scar tissue on my brain returned as intensely as before. It used to be so strong that I would black out. It was somewhat like somebody thrust a knife right down through my skull into my brain where the scar tissue was growing. The pain shot into my brain. The scar tissue was a growth on my brain which became inflamed at times. It's like a swelling condition of the brain. As it grows, it causes this intense pain. The pain that came after I was healed felt just a little different, but it appeared the same. I learned to identify the difference in the feeling. I learned to quickly recognize the voice of Satan. I knew the difference between the way Jesus spoke and the way Satan spoke. I learned after my healing that the devil and all his helpers talked to me just as real as when I talk to my family. As soon as I had this pain, here would come a whole flood of doubt and fear into my mind, just as plain as if they were saying, "You know you're not really healed."

The whole five weeks was a battle of, "Am I going to believe what God said He had done, or am I going to believe all this other gossip that is coming into my head?"

I constantly prayed, praised God and testified of the healing.

These attacks went from very severe the first week to less and less and less until at the end of five weeks there was hardly any trouble. It seemed like the devil let go gradually, or else the Word became so much more real to me, and the victory became so much more real that I didn't hear what he was saying.

Even after years had passed, once in a great while I'll have a short visit from the devil. Recently a wave of numbness flowed over my body and the devil said, "See, you're getting sick again; your healing of M.S. was just a remission." I prayed, rebuked it in Jesus' name, and went on about my business for Jesus, and it left right away. If a symptom of stiffness or something else related to the signs of MS or a thought about it comes into my mind, I quote the Word, *"I shall not die, but live, and declare the works of the Lord."* I go right on with what I am doing at the time and have no more trouble.

Another portion of scripture that has been important to me when these thoughts come into my mind is II Corinthians 10:3-5:

"For though we walk in the flesh, we do not war after the flesh: For the weapons of our warfare are not carnal, but mighty through God to the pulling down of strong holds; casting down imaginations, and every high thing that exalteth itself against the knowledge of God, and bringing into captivity every thought to the obedience of Christ" (KJV).

The attacks by thought have been as severe as the attacks by symptoms of illness, but by the Word of God and the power of the Holy Spirit, I have brought into captivity every thought to the obedience of Christ. Every thought the devil has put into my mind has been replaced with what the Word of God says.

The prayers, the Word, the fellowship with those who believe in healing, the praises to God and the confessing of the healing, giving the glory to God, are so important.

I believe if a person is healed, he should do everything possible to be around believers, especially during the early period following the healing. He should be in church where healings frequently occur so he will be in an atmosphere of belief. My friends and my church stood close by me during my first trying five weeks. Sometimes a family will not even believe when the evidence of healing is present. Little do they realize that their unbelief may cause their loved one to return to suffering and death. Jesus saw unbelief at work when He returned to His home town. He only did a few miracles because of unbelief.

When a person gives his life to Jesus and is born again, his priorities change. He can go on, like I chose to do, and serve Jesus, or he can return to his old ways of sinning, like I did so many years. Priorities of desires, activities, habits and environment must change or the devil will come to steal and kill. He wants to defeat our healing the same way. But Jesus is the winner if we do our part!

The night I went to the Hunter meeting, I knew before I went that when I was prayed for, I was going to be healed. I also knew that it wouldn't be any different five weeks later, because I knew that was what the Lord had for me. I had read it in His Word, and I believed. I still believe and always will, because, *"I shall not die, but live, and declare the works of the Lord."**

If you have never read Dodie Osteen's book, Healed of Cancer, it is a must for everyone who is battling cancer. "Dodie was diagnosed on Thursday, December 10, 1981. John Osteen was told the following devastating news. The doctors said, 'Pastor, your wife has metastatic cancer of the liver. With or without chemotherapy, she has only a few weeks to live. We can treat her, but it will only slightly prolong her life.'

"'However, we cannot find the primary tumor,' he said. 'We don't know where it is. In fact, it has really baffled us. Usually a primary tumor signifies the beginning of cancer and then it spreads to the liver or kidneys or some place else. But we cannot find one. With your consent, we would like to do exploratory surgery or a colonoscopy to try to locate the tumor.'

"John couldn't believe it. He said, 'Doctor, I am going to take my wife home. We are going to pray and seek God, and then we will decide what to do. We believe in miracles, and we believe in the Miracle Worker.'

"The doctor said, 'Well, Pastor, you're going to have to have a miracle this time.'" Dodie went home on December 10, 1981 and never went back to the hospital. John anointed her with oil the day after she got home from the hospital! As they were both on the floor in their bedroom, face down before God, he took authority over any disease and over all cancerous cells in her body.

Dodie says, "As far as I'm concerned, that's the day my healing began." Dodie fought the symptoms and the attacks of the devil for five years – five long years, but her faith never wavered and even though it was not an instant miracle it started on the day when she and John made a covenant that her healing had started. Don't get discouraged. Today, fifteen years later, she is a beautiful woman, a picture of health.

One of my favorite stories about Dodie Osteen's healing is this:

"When I was sick, I would look at two pictures of me in radiant health – one in my wedding dress and one riding a horse on a ranch. They bolstered my faith and helped me keep a positive attitude – especially when I was feeling so sick.

"I kept looking at those pictures and saying, 'Thank

You, Father, that You will restore health to me and heal me of my wounds. I thank You that I'll feel like I did when I married at 21. I'll feel like I did when I was 25 riding that horse. I thank You that You will restore me to health, Father.'

"When I started feeling good again, I said, 'Father, thank You that You have restored health to me.' I repeat this often – even now!"

It was a miracle of God regardless of how you look at it!

Don't get discouraged if you don't see an instant miracle. Some miracles happen the moment you lay hands on the sick – but other healings take time. Tell the person to whom you are ministering that the healing has started once you have laid hands on them. Do everything you can to keep people from becoming discouraged. Build their faith – and yours – with every sentence you speak.

We do not lay hands on the sick when we feel like it. We lay hands on the sick at every opportunity! Some of the greatest healings we have ever seen have taken place when we were sick or completely exhausted. Don't wait for a feeling – do it now!

When God opens a door for you, go through it. He always has something special for you on the other side. Freely you have received, freely give!

If an opportunity to lay hands on someone occurs – go for it – regardless of whether you feel anything or not.

You'll be in the miracle ministry, too!

Chapter Sixteen

Miracles Began To Happen – Immediately!

Renée Branson has been the anointed secretary for John Osteen, pastor of the great Lakewood Church in Houston, Texas, for 15 years. She has sat under his outstanding teaching all of these precious years and is so full of the Word that it literally pours out of her constantly. She is a total delight to be around at all times, but you'll be thrilled to see what happened when she believed, "If Charles and Frances can do it, you can do it, too!"

In November 1994 during a week of vacation time I decided to visit Charles and Frances Hunter's ministry office because I was interested in their miracle ministry. They graciously spent two hours with me and gave me a lot of teaching material including their 15-hour tape series on "How To Heal The Sick". That week of vacation I watched those teaching tapes hour after hour, taking 30 pages of notes, and God deposited so much in me that literally changed the course of my life and ministry. Immediately miracles began to happen as I put into practice what I had learned.

I believe one of the greatest things I learned was that I was not waiting on God to do something – He was waiting on me to do something! I learned God was not the one limiting me, but that I was limiting Him. I learned that when we obey The Great Commission to go, preach, teach, heal, cast out demons, and help people receive the baptism in the Holy Spirit, that Jesus will work with us to confirm His Word with signs following.

The second most important thing I learned from the tapes was to quickly categorize a person's ailment into one of three categories so that I could apply healing in a specific way to get results. I remember the shocking statement the Hunters made that "Jesus never prayed for the sick." They explained that Jesus healed by "speaking and laying hands on people." I learned that there are a great variety of ways to heal the sick, and that Jesus healed people primarily in three specific ways.

1) Jesus spoke to people's bodies and they were healed.

2) Jesus spoke creative miracles, calling the things that be not as though they were.

3) Jesus spoke to demons to loose people's bodies.

I was amazed watching the tapes how the human body responds to a spoken command of authority given in the name of the Jesus and by the power of the Holy Spirit. To me this was the main key to unlocking the miracle-working power of God. When I spoke "in the name of Jesus" I was recognizing His authority over sickness and disease and every name that is named. And when I said, "and by the power of the Holy Spirit", I was acknowledging that miracles are the work of the Holy Spirit who lives in me and gives me the same "dunamis" power to work miracles that Jesus had. I saw creative miracles on the tapes that increased my faith. I also learned that the majority of what the world calls "incurable" diseases are caused by demons attacking a person's body, and that when you bind the demon and free the person from its influence, they begin immediately to amend.

One particular illustration Charles used in the tapes helped me to really understand the power of God and how it is available to every believer 24 hours a day. He explained that as a generator of electricity makes electrical power available continuously so that when a person goes to a wall switch and turns it on, the power from the generator is free to flow to illuminate a light bulb—just so, the Holy Spirit (the power) that lives in our spirit (the generator), makes His power available to us 24 hours a day, so that when we (the wall switch) lay hands on the sick (connecting the power), the person is healed (the light bulb illuminates). Then I fully understood that the Holy Spirit makes God's healing power available to me continually to use whenever there is a need. I also learned that healing is not just in our hands, but that we are anointed from head to toe!

Another valuable lesson I learned from watching the tapes was when ministering to people to EXPECT something to happen – after all, you are literally releasing God's power into people when you speak to them and/or lay hands on them. They said if what you do doesn't work, then try something else; listen to the instruction of the Holy Spirit inside your spirit and learn to cooperate with Him as He teaches you what to do. They said it is important to get people to act and begin to do what they could not do before so they can see that God has truly healed them. The Hunters' childlike faith in God's ability and willingness to heal left an indelible mark in my mind and heart.

The Hunters did not just teach about healing on the tapes; they demonstrated the power of God as God confirmed His Word with signs following. I saw actual healing miracles on the tapes. I learned that when I said what I heard Charles and Frances say, and did what I saw Charles and Frances do, I got the same results. They constantly said, "If Charles and Frances can do it, you can do it, too."

Some practical things I learned included that pain, if not explained by some medical reason, was caused by a spirit of pain that would leave immediately when rebuked. Only three weeks after watching the healing videos, I rebuked a spirit of pain in a man's shoulder and it left immediately. He had not been able to raise his arm above his head due to pain for several months, but was able immediately to raise his arm high over his head with no pain whatsoever!

I learned that 80% of all people have back problems and that a large portion of people's ailments are due to spinal injuries. I learned injuries to the upper spine affect the eyes, ears, nose, face, and throat; injuries to the middle part of the spine affect the major organs in the body; injuries to the lower spine and pelvis affect the lower parts of the body. I learned there are 100,000 nerves that are located at each disc between the vertebrae that when damaged can cause other body parts to malfunction.

I learned to command the discs, vertebrae, as well as the nerves, muscles, ligaments and tendons connected to them, to line up perfectly in the spinal column and to be the proper length and strength.

I learned that a misaligned pelvic bone can be tilted too far backward or too far forward, be tilted with one hip higher than the other, be turned too far outward, or too far inward, causing such things as a sway back, straight back, curvature of the spine, bowlegs, or pigeon-toes, one leg or arm shorter than the other, and a variety of problems such as pain, bedwetting, female trouble, bowel problems, etc. I learned that commanding the pelvic bone to shift into place in the name of Jesus and by the power of the Holy Spirit causes the miracle-working power of God to go to work immediately to correct the position of the pelvic bone and bring it back into perfect alignment in the body, healing the affected parts of the body! As I have ministered this healing technique I have personally seen more miracles of healing in the back and pelvic areas than any other area.

I heard Frances say on the tapes that women can give birth supernaturally to their children by asking God to oil the birth canal with the oil of the Holy Spirit and to give birth within three hours with no pain. Recently our church staff prayed this for two of our staff members who were expecting babies, and both gave birth within three hours with minimal discomfort!

During the past two years since viewing the "How To Heal the Sick" video tapes, I have been sharing the information I learned with ladies groups, churches, and Bible school students. I have also told them, "If I can do it, you can do it, too!" Those people who believe what I preach, teach, and demonstrate, and began to practice what they see and hear, are now seeing miracles, too. If they can do it, you can do it!

I saw Charles minister the baptism with the Holy

Spirit to a group all at one time on the tapes and decided I could do it, too. I did it and group after group has been filled with the Holy Ghost, speaking in other tongues.

Let me share some of the outstanding miracles out of the hundreds where I have personally ministered healing to encourage you to believe God for great manifestations of His healing power through you as a believer.

In a meeting in Corpus Christi a mother brought an 18-month old baby for prayer who had one straight leg and one very crooked, arched leg in a half-moon shape. The baby was facing a series of corrective surgeries to straighten out the leg so it would be straight like the other one. I felt impressed by the Holy Ghost to lay my hand on the baby's little pelvic bone, which I did, and I commanded it to rotate outward in the name of Jesus and by the power of the Holy Spirit. I watched in amazement as the deformed leg straightened out completely right in front of my eyes, and was perfectly parallel to the other leg in less than five seconds! Wow!

I was in a ladies meeting in Kilgore, Texas when a woman with rheumatoid arthritis came for prayer. Her hands were so deformed, twisted and gnarled that her hands which were turned to the outside of her body at the wrists were clamped shut with swelling, and her fingers pointed upwards at the middle knuckles toward the backs of her hands!

I laid hands on her and rebuked the spirit of arthritis in the name of Jesus and by the power of the Holy Spirit. Then I commanded her closed fist to open up. Nothing happened, but I knew something should be happening. Suddenly, I heard myself say by the Holy Ghost (this thought never entered my mind), "You, foul, crippling spirit, in the na..." Suddenly the power of God began to flow into her hands like a river and the hands began to open from a clenched position very dramatically. As I continued to use the name of Jesus, the swollen knuckles and wrist bones on both hands that were three times their normal size reduced in size by one-half. Her fingers that were bent backward and blue on the tips, due to the circulation being cut off, began to straighten out very slowly. As I commanded the circulation to be restored, the fingertips on both hands became pink instantly! Then I commanded the hands which were turned at the wrists to straighten up and be aligned at the end of her arms, and they did! This miracle was like watching a 30-minute time-lapse photography film. It was very dramatic, and beautiful to watch the Holy Spirit work!

Recently a woman came for prayer who had a horrible wound in her hand. She said she had diabetes and the wound would not heal. The wound began at the center of her palm and fanned outward to a width of 1/2-inch in the middle of the outside edge of the hand under her little finger. It was 1/8-inch deep, split open, dried and bloody, and very painful. I laid my hands on her, bound the spirit of diabetes and commanded it to leave her. Then I spoke a creative miracle and asked God to give her a new pancreas. Next, I held her hand in mine and prayed for the healing virtue of the Lord Jesus Christ to flow into her hand and restore her flesh like that of a little child. I knew in the natural that it would take from three to six months of care at a special wound care center for a deep wound of that nature to heal. I was shocked when the woman came only eleven days later and the hand was totally healed with no discoloration whatsoever! The only evidence the wound had been there was a tiny bluish-white hairline mark that looked like an old scar at one place on the outside edge of her hand. Praise the Lord!

I say along with Charles and Frances Hunter, if we can do it, you can do it, too!

(Renée Branson)

Chapter Seventeen

Spare Parts Department

God has a warehouse of spare parts! God made you and He is smarter than General Motors. General Motors has spare parts for all of their automobiles. God has new parts for you, too.

A girl heard me say one time that God has a warehouse of spare parts and she said "I'm not sure I believe that." She had rheumatic fever when she was a young girl and it left her with a bad heart. She heard me tell how God had given me a new heart. That's been 22 years ago now, and so she said, "God, would you just let me see a heavenly warehouse so I know that you really have got spare parts."

If each of us were to figure in our own mind what the warehouse looked like, we would all think of something different as to what the spare parts department in heaven looks like. Maybe if you're a mechanic you would see shelves like you do in these automobile places where they have parts in all these little different spaces. I always thought about the spare parts department in heaven as being like a freezer or meat cooler in a grocery store where they have big hooks with beef carcasses hanging on them. I could see hearts hanging up there and all kinds of spare parts. But this girl said, "God, let me see what a warehouse of spare parts is."

She was so amazed she said, "I still don't know if it was a dream or a vision or what it was, but suddenly I saw a river of water clear as crystal flowing out of the throne room of God. It was icy cold and beautifully clear and there were some objects just bouncing up and down all over." She said, "I looked a little closer and it was hearts! All hearts and they were in this cold, clear water." She was fascinated watching all these hearts go by when suddenly one appeared that had the name "Susie" on it. She said, "I'll take it!" And as she grabbed for the heart with the name "Susie" on it, she was instantly healed by the power of God!

It's the same as a retread on a car. You see them all over the highways. Get a new part – not a retread. Charles and I never ask for a repair job on people. If you've got something that's worn out we always ask for a new one.

I received an interesting fax down in Mexico on my birthday. It was from the president of Channel 40 TV station in Pittsburgh. He said, "Frances, since your heart is less than 25 years old and your thyroid is 30 years old and your pancreas is 12 years old and your blood system is 8, how much of the original Frances Hunter is there left to wish happy birthday?" Hallelujah!

I said to Charles, "I'd have a difficult time dying because all my parts are different ages." Some are real young and some are slightly old. Some I've got are the original ones but don't hesitate to ask God for a new part because He has a great supply!

The Word of God tells us that we can call into being those things which be not as though they were and we have seen some incredible things happen as we have called into being new hearts, new livers, new stomachs and many other parts. Remember when you''re praying for the sick you have absolutely nothing to lose because you can't do anything to make them worse, all you can do is leave them in an improved or healed position.

Over the years many, many people have come up to us and will say something similar to this: "You laid hands on me 15 years ago for a new heart and I received a new heart and have never had a problem from that day to this!"

These are not the type of healings that you can tell about instantly because there's no way that we can look on the inside of you and see whether or not you have received a new heart, a new liver or any other organ, but time will tell and it's such a delight to us to have people come up as somebody just recently did and say, "You laid hands on me 26 years ago for a new liver. I was dying of cancer and my liver was swollen and distended but you laid hands on me and within two months the cancer had totally disappeared and the liver was absolutely normal." What rejoicing there was in my heart because this also proves that God's healings last. Many people are inclined to believe that people just get "hyped up" in services and that the healings will disappear as soon as they get home. This is totally untrue because God's healings will last unless we do something to bring the same thing back upon us. They will stand up under an X-ray or blood test!

Try calling into being some new parts that you may need or someone else may need and see what happens. You will be delighted, especially with the first doctor's diagnosis that says, "I don't understand what happened, but you have a new heart!"

Remember if Charles and Frances can do it, you can do it too, and that means calling into being new parts in the name of Jesus.

Chapter Eighteen
The Endocrine System

It is helpful to know the location and purpose of the endocrine system.

The endocrine system is a complex system of glands that produce and secrete hormones directly into the circulatory system to influence, regulate and control metabolism and many of the body's processes.

1. **Pineal:** cone-shaped gland at the base of the brain that secretes the hormone melatonin, which may help to synchronize biorhythms and mark the passage of time.

2. **Pituitary:** the body's "master gland," which stimulates the adrenals, thyroid, pigmentation-producing skin cells and gonads. Also secretes growth hormone, the antidiuretic hormone prolactin, and oxytocin, a hormone that causes contractions of the uterus during labor.

3. **Thyroid:** produces the hormones thyroxine, triiodothyronine, and calcitonin, which stimulate metabolism, body heat production and bone growth.

4. **Parathyroid:** endocrine glands whose hormones regulate the use and function of calcium and phosphorus in the body.

5. **Thymus:** gland located behind the breastbone that is important in the development of cell-mediated

immune responses.

6. **Adrenals:** release hydro-cortisone, which effects metabolism. Also produce androgen hormones and aldosterone hormone, which maintains blood pressure and the body's salt and potassium balance.

7. **Pancreas:** abdominal organ, secretes insulin and glucagon, which control the utilization of sugar, the body's chief source of energy.

8. **Ovaries (not shown):** female glands that produce the hormones estrogen and progesterone, which influence female physiology.

9. **Testes (not shown):** male glands secrete testosterone, which stimulates sperm production and development of male characteristics.*

If you will study this chart carefully it will assist you greatly to know where an individual's problems are located, then you can lay hands on the approximate area designated by the various numbers.

*SOURCE: Chicago Tribune, AMA Encyclopedia of Medicine

Chapter Nineteen

You'd Never Believe It!

Jim and Helen Bishop are two people you would never suspect (if you looked at them in the natural) to accomplish the things they do. Both are over seventy years old but they have a desire to be obedient and to please Jesus. The following testimony was received from them and we're inserting it with absolutely no changes. They are not well educated people, they are not wealthy people, they are just people who love Jesus with their mind, their heart, their body and their soul and who believed that if Charles and Frances can do it, you can do it too. Look what they have accomplished.

The charter we got, patterned after yours, has born much fruit!

We ordained a man named Lou Castriota, who had a dozen folks in a prayer group.

They quickly grew into a group (40) who are doing free give-aways in parks, with meals, groceries, prayer for salvation, healing, baptism, etc.

This Saturday, they are going to be seven locations where folks from Catholic, Protestant and Episcopal churches band together. No arguments, no striving for memberships, just the Word and "Jesus Loves You," on their lips.

It's an all day affair, food, clothing, music, prayers, even some free haircuts!

It's a miracle and it spawned from Miracle Ministry, (ours) from YOUR ministry.

There is also a weekly group who go to a poor black neighborhood every Friday night and do the same thing there. We have drunks, dope addicts, prostitutes and discouraged people come and eat and listen to the prayers.

Some stay for counselling, some get saved and some get healed and bring friends the next week. It's on a double parking lot of a "Resource Center," no facilities, they sit on the parking bumpers and some chairs.

The group doing all this is called "New Beginnings." Indeed it is, for many.

At the all day affairs monthly we have security police and county booths for crisis helps.

A black Pentecostal church is using our preachers. We all went there Sunday and the place was "shaken." They loved us. The word was preached, several got healed and joy was there.

YOU can do it, too!

(Jim and Helen Bishop)

Chapter Twenty
It Works in Every Nation

It doesn't matter what language you speak, whether it's English, Spanish, Russian, Korean or any other language in the world, the Word of God works wherever you are. It doesn't just work in sections, it works all the way whether you're talking about healing and health, prosperity, peace of mind and heart, the Word of God works through any language in the world!

On January 1, 1996 I (Frances) received a phone call from Acapulco, Mexico. The caller said, "Frances, how would you like to celebrate your 80th birthday with a healing explosion in Acapulco?" The Holy Spirit quickened me and my answer immediately came back, "Yes, I would love to celebrate my birthday that way!" That was the start of one of the most incredible healing explosions we have ever had in our entire lives. The first training session was a great surprise because they had to take it outdoors to an amphitheater because the crowd was so large and instead of a crowd between 800 and 900 they had over 2,400 at the first training session and learn they did!

When the night came for the actual healing explosion the faith of the people had risen so high because of the miracles they had seen happen during the training sessions, and believing what we said was true, "if Charles and Frances can do it, you can do it too," they attacked the sick people with an aggressiveness that we had never seen up until that time.

We asked the people who were healed to come up on the stage and tell what they were healed of and before long we had a line of 100 people testifying as to what God had done for them or for their children. Several mothers were ecstatic as they reported, "My little girl or my little boy has never walked in her or his entire life. Look at him or her run." We would look and see a little child running all over the stage who had never walked in their entire life. We would ask them who did the healing and they would say, "I don't know." They would then suddenly realize it was Jesus but not an individual anywhere there.

For at least two hours we had between one and two hundred people on the stage testifying as rapidly as they could about their healing. We had to have two translators because it was such a huge work that it would have worn out one translator. So, we had to have two who took the people one right after another one. All of these miracles were done through ordinary believers.

It was heartbreaking to us to have people come up and say, "I was blind but now I see" and we didn't even have time to find out what had caused their blindness or how long they had been blind, all we could say is, "Great, next." We had such a line up on the stage that it was impossible to spend much time with anyone.

When the lights went off at midnight or thereabouts there was still a line of over 100 people waiting to get up and to testify what God had done! When people come with such tremendous faith as they came to those meetings, it's so easy for anyone to lay hands on the sick and see the incredible miracles happen.

The people on the healing teams said that the power of God was so strong in the area where the people came down to receive healing that they didn't even get to lay hands on a lot of them before they got healed. Approximately 45 people from the United States had gone to Acapulco to be a part of this celebration and they said the same thing that they had never seen such a display of the awesome power of God.

One young man who had very poor eyesight sent his sunglasses up and he said, "I just know if somebody lays hands on them, I'll be able to see perfectly." Hands were laid on his sunglasses and they were sent back to him and his sight was instantly greatly improved! You don't have to be a "star" to see incredible healings, you just have to be obedient. Remember, if Charles and Frances can do it, you can do it too, even if you speak Spanish.

Often people ask us, "How do you stay so excited all the time about Jesus?" There is only one reason: Christianity is not a religion, it is a way of life that you live 24 hours out of every day. Remember always that Christ in you is the hope of glory! Start believing that He is actually living inside of you and that when you stretch forth your hand, that's the hand of Jesus to be laid on the sick. The more this becomes a living reality in our lives, the more all of us can accomplish for the kingdom of God, regardless of where we live or what language we speak. We don't believe the people in Acapulco will ever be the same again!

Russia is an incredible place!

Three years ago we went to Kiev, which is the bread basket of Russia, and taught the people how to minister healing to the sick. We do not know of any other country where they were so hungry to learn this wonderful ability that God has given to all of us. When Jesus said, *"Those who believe will lay hands on the sick,"* that's exactly what He meant. You just have to be a believer, be obedient, and then get out and do it.

At the first healing explosion in Kiev, we had many of the children who suffered birth defects as a result of the Chernoble explosion. Many of these children are blind in one eye and many of them are crippled but what an exciting thing to see these children come up on the stage and be able to see with two eyes because one of the Ukrainians had laid hands on them and they were healed! Many children who had never walked were running around the auditorium that day because somebody believed that they could lay hands upon the sick and see them recover! And they did!

There was a very exciting aftermath to the two healing explosions! Four months later we went back to the Ukraine again. As we visited various churches, they would bring three or four people who were critically ill and who had come out from the hospital for us to lay hands on and as soon as we laid hands on them, then the pastor would say to us, "Now, we want you two to sit down and watch and see what we have learned!"

We could hardly believe what we were seeing. These Ukrainian people are so aggressive in laying hands on the sick that we saw incredible miracles as we sat down and watched these Ukrainians do it.

In church after church we saw exactly the same thing and had the same request from the pastor, "You sit down so we can show you what we have learned." How it thrills our hearts to see the body of Christ in any country come alive and become aware of the fact that God can use them!

The Soul of Korea

What a wild exciting time a very recent trip to Seoul, Korea was! We spoke for three days at a Presbyterian pastors' meeting, attended by pastors from all over Korea.

Of the crowd of over 1,000 pastors and their wives, not more than ten had received the baptism with the Holy Spirit. We spoke the first night on the Holy Ghost and Fire – Catch It! When we made the call for the baptism with the Holy Spirit, no one was more surprised than we were at the response. They had listened to every word we said and every bit of teaching that we did in the Word on the baptism with the Holy Spirit and all but about fifty responded to the call for the baptism with the Holy Spirit. They continued responding as we started to minister the baptism with the Holy Spirit, and an additional forty came forward. There were only about ten people left in their seats! We assumed that these had already received.

As Charles ministered the baptism with the Holy Spirit and they all began to speak with other tongues, there was a sound that went through the entire auditorium that was not like any sound we had ever heard in all of our lives! The rushing mighty wind of the Holy Spirit made a sound in the most powerful manner you could ever imagine as they all began to speak with other tongues!

The morning teaching sessions on How To Heal The Sick were unbelievable because of the awesome response and hunger of the pastors to learn how to minister healing.

On the final morning session, after the healing teaching, we had them hold hands in the pews because we wanted to give them a special anointing for healing and since we had laid hands on all of them for the fire of God the first night we decided to run down the aisles and touch the hand of the person on the end of the pew.

They went under the power in rows! It was like ocean waves!

People who were in the middle of the pews said they never realized that the anointing could reach so far in and touch them! One of them said that it was just like a ball of fire hit them in the stomach as we ran down the aisles.

The final service was "The Charge," and afterwards, we said, "Now, we give you your first opportunity to do what God said to do." We commissioned the eleven pastors who were up for the Charge and some of the other leaders to stand up and to start laying hands on the sick.

It was one of the most unbelievable sights that you could ever imagine as these pastors who never had the baptism with the Holy Spirit, who never even dreamed that healing was for today, were laying hands on people! People were being healed and going out under the power of God all over the auditorium.

The pastors had an incredible time! God is raising up tremendous leaders in Korea. That nation will never be the same!

    If they can do it in Korea, you can do it, too!

Chapter Twenty-One

Seven Steps To Ministering Healing

Jesus said: *"Go into all the world and preach the gospel to every creature. He who believes and is baptized will be saved; but he who does not believe will be condemned"* (Mark 16:15-16).

Step 1: Believe What The Word Of God Says

"And these signs will follow those who <u>believe</u>: In My name they will cast out demons; they will speak with new tongues; they will take up serpents; and if they drink anything deadly, it will by no means hurt them; they will lay hands on the sick, and they will recover" (Mark 16:17-18).

I repeat these last eleven words: *"They will lay hands on the sick, and they will recover."* It is imperative that we believe with all our hearts that His desire is for believers to lay hands on the sick with results.

We must also believe Philippians 2:9-11: *"Therefore God also has highly exalted Him and given Him the name which is above every name, that at the name of Jesus every knee should bow, of those in heaven, and of those on earth, and of those under the earth, and that every tongue should confess that Jesus Christ is Lord, to the glory of God the Father."*

The name of Jesus is above the name of every disease that exists or which will ever exist. It is above the name of cancer, arthritis, cerebral palsy, Parkinson's disease, or any other disease.

Sometimes when we're first obedient to Jesus and lay hands on the sick, we approach the power that is in the name of Jesus, *asking*, "In the name of Jesus?" Instead we should approach healing with absolute confidence in the power that is in that very special name.

I made a very interesting typographical mistake when I typed the original notes for this book. I had planned to type "medi*tate* in the Bible"; instead I had typed "medi*cate* in the Bible." I laughed as I started to correct the error. But the more I thought about it, the more I realized that the Bible is medicine to our minds, bodies, souls and spirits. The more you medicate on the Word, the more you will be convinced that God heals today.

Nothing will keep us as strong as God's Word, and nothing will help in healing more than the Word. When you "medicate" on the Word of God, it will heal you of any unbelief. To be successful in the healing ministry, you must get rid of unbelief when the devil constantly tries to put questions about healing in your mind. It is amazing to see what happens when you give the Word to someone to whom you are ministering healing.

I remember the day I was healed of diabetes. Not realizing that God had healed me, I was still taking my insulin and went into insulin shock in the Atlanta airport. As I fell over in the chair, my Bible opened to Psalm 30:2, which says, *"O Lord my God, I cried out to You, and You have healed me."*

I moaned, "But I don't feel like it."

I repeated the verse again, *"O Lord my God, I cried out to You, and You have healed me."* I moaned again, "But I don't feel like it."

"O Lord my God, I cried out to You, and You have healed me." I moaned again, "But I don't feel like it."

After I had said that about ten times, suddenly the truth of what had happened dawned on me. I screamed, *"'O Lord my God, I cried out to You, and You have healed me,'* and because I've got a new pancreas and am taking artificial insulin, I have gone into insulin shock!" I screamed for Charles to get me some sugar or some orange juice because I knew that was the only thing that would bring me out of it. Shortly after he brought me some candy, I felt fine! The same doctor who diagnosed my diabetes two weeks earlier re-examined me and said, "You have a new pancreas, so throw away your medicine!"

I knew right then and there that I had been totally healed of diabetes. I haven't had a problem or sign of diabetes from that day to this. I believe that what God does, He does well. *"He hath done all things well" (Mark 7:37, KJV).*

There's power in God's Word. That Scripture passage in the airport gave me something to cling to. It let me know beyond any shadow of doubt that I was healed.

In 1988 I was healed of endocarditis (the inflammation of the lining of the heart and its valves). At that time God gave me another verse. The doctors had told me I wasn't going to live because my blood system was pulling off pieces of my heart. They gave me four days, possibly longer with massive doses of antibiotics. We had often prayed, "Father, when You show us what the problem is, we will know how to pray for Frances."

Charles simply laid hands on my heart and commanded, "In Jesus' name, I command a new blood system!" That was what the Holy Spirit first put into his mind to pray, and that is what I needed. They said that when enough heart tissue had been destroyed, my life would end. The night after Charles prayed for me, a supernatural event took place right in our bedroom.

Although in my spirit I did not receive the diagnosis the doctors had given me, Charles took me to a heart specialist in Houston who ordered additional tests.

When we returned home, I was exhausted and fell into a sound sleep.

I was awakened in the middle of the night and felt as if I had been hit on the head and chest by a large piece of wood. While I do not know if it was a vision or a dream, it was one of the most real things I have ever experienced in my entire life!

I looked, and there, completely covering my chest, appeared to be a huge, wooden book. On it was one single verse of Scripture:

"Those who wait on the Lord
Shall renew their strength;
They shall mount up with wings like eagles,
They shall run and not be weary,
They shall walk and not faint" (Is. 40:31).

Instantly, in that split second of time when God gave me that verse, I knew that I knew that I knew that I had been healed, because God had renewed my strength!

Many Scripture passages will give you confidence if you will remember them when you are laying hands on the sick. They are also beneficial to you in the event you yourself should ever need healing.

Hebrews 4:12 - "For the word of God is living and powerful, and sharper than any two-edged sword, piercing even to the division of soul and spirit, and of joints and marrow, and is a discerner of the thoughts and intents of the heart."

We need not fear disease, because the Word of God is so sharp that it can cut through any disease or crippling situation in which we might find ourselves.

Isaiah 55:11 - "So shall My word be that goes forth from My mouth; it shall not return to Me void, but it shall accomplish what I please, and it shall prosper in the thing for which I sent it."

God sends His Word "on an assignment" to heal if we believe and command!

Luke 11:28 - "Blessed are those who hear the word of God and keep it!"

Not only do we need to hear it, but we also need to keep it. You can be blessed just by hearing it, but you can be more than doubly blessed by hearing it and keeping it!

Mark 13:31 - "Heaven and earth will pass away, but My words will by no means pass away."

What a powerful comfort to know that His Words will never pass away. You can rest assured that this is a fact which will never change.

Romans 10:17 - "So then faith comes by hearing, and hearing by the word of God."

At times this is the written Word of God, but often it's the rhema word that God speaks into your heart. You know that you have heard from God when He gives you that special word, and that it will come to pass in your life.

Psalm 119:11 - "Your word I have hidden in my heart, that I might not sin against You."

When that old nature comes up in us, giving us an urge to sin, we need to remember, *"Your word I have hidden in my heart, that I might not sin against You."* It is amazing how fast the remembrance of that verse will keep us from crossing over the line into sin again!

Luke 4:4 - "It is written, 'Man shall not live by bread alone, but by every word of God.'"

Every, not just part, but by every word of God.

Step 2: Make Healing a Life-Style

Catch a vision of what God has called you to do. Then go out and do it! It goes beyond putting on a hat on Sunday mornings, going to church and, when the service is over, thinking, "Well, I did my little thing for the week, so here I go!" Then you go out the door and live just as you did previously, coming back the following Sunday, thinking that you're living the Christian life-style.

Real Christianity is a life-style that you live every moment of every day. There's no time off, no vacation time, because it's a twenty-four-hour-a-day thing, every day of the year.

I got saved at the ripe old age of forty-nine, and I went up like a rocket. I left the church that morning and tried to beat Jesus into the head of every person I met. I went up and down U.S. Highway 1 in Kendall, Florida, like a wild woman. And I was wild about Jesus!

When I went to church the next Sunday, I was excited because of all the wonderful things that had happened during my first week as a Christian. I started out the first day to make Christianity a life-style. I shocked many of the "old" saints in the church who promptly said: "She'll never make it; she'll fizzle out. She won't last long. Those who go up like that come down real fast, and then they crash."

It's been more than thirty-two years, and I'm still going strong, and I intend to keep on going stronger until Jesus returns. Peculiarly, many of those "saints" have backslidden since then. It has caused me to wonder about something.

What makes a person hang in there with God? What makes a person fizzle out? What makes a person hang in there with healing? Many times at a healing explosion we see people get so excited that they want to lay hands on everyone in sight. You see them laying hands on the sick in the hotel elevators. You see them growing out waiters' and waitresses' arms. But the important thing is not what they do at a healing explosion, but what they will do to keep from fizzling out once the Healing Explosion is over.

Charles and I have made healing a life-style. Everywhere we go we lay hands on the sick. We talk about Jesus and what He wants us Christians to do now! We don't talk about anything else.

We don't feel anything else is worth talking about.

The other night in a cafeteria a man came up to us and asked if we minded the interruption. After we assured him that we did not, he said, "Fifteen years ago you laid hands on me for deliverance from cigarettes.

"Although I haven't seen you from that day to this, I've never smoked another cigarette since."

What a whoop-and-holler time we had right there in

the cafeteria. To me that is exciting news and I'm sure there wasn't another conversation in the cafeteria nearly as exciting as ours. We praised the Lord right there in public because it is a life-style with us. It's not something that we pretend to have in the pulpit. It's something we do every waking moment of our day.

The excitement of our first week of salvation needs to be part of our walk with Jesus right now. We should all notice the needs of others whether we are in a grocery store, at work or in the church. Those people need you and me to help them find the answer to life.

The day I got saved I made a decision, a quality decision, and nothing could ever make me change my mind.

I made an everlasting decision.

We must not vacillate. We need to get into the Bible, our holding power, instead of saying, "I don't think this 'stuff' works!" or, "I'm not sure I can cope with this."

Think how much worse it would be if you didn't have the answer to cope with problems!

Recently Charles and I went to a conference where the main topic was survival. We've never heard so much gloom and doom in our entire lives. Charles and I are looking forward to the best years of our lives, though we're older than we have ever been before! We're looking forward not just to surviving, but to living the abundant life Jesus promised. We have a purpose – doing the works of Jesus!

Wherever you go, Jesus always provides opportunities to minister in His name.

One day a man came into our office to see about some concrete work we needed. He had never seen a miracle, but before he got out of there, he saw his own leg grow out in divine healing. He was already saved, but he went on to receive the baptism with the Holy Spirit, which he had been seeking for years.

He walked out a different person! Sometimes we think that we shouldn't talk about Jesus to people with whom we do business because we think they might not be interested or because we think "business is business." I personally believe Jesus is the best business to talk about, and that's why we discuss Him all the time.

When God planted a seed in you, He did not plant that seed to die. He planted that seed to grow in you.

You apparently have something inside of you that makes you want to heal the sick, or else you would not be reading this book. God has dropped a seed into your heart, and you need to nurture that seed and get a vision of what God has called you to do. Ignore circumstances that might try to change your mind.

Step 3: Have Confidence in God In You

It's easy to have confidence in God, because nothing is impossible with God. We all know He can do anything. We know He can heal the sickest person; through God the most crippled person can be healed and walk perfectly. But do we believe God can use us? We need to have confidence in God in us.

In Matthew 17:14-20 we read:

"And when they had come to the multitude, a man came to Him, kneeling down to Him and saying, 'Lord, have mercy on my son, for he is an epileptic and suffers severely; for he often falls into the fire and often into the water. So I brought him to Your disciples, but they could not cure him.'

"Then Jesus answered and said, 'O faithless and perverse generation, how long shall I be with you? How long shall I bear with you? Bring him here to Me.' And Jesus rebuked the demon, and he came out of him; and the child was cured from that very hour.

"Then the disciples came to Jesus privately and said, 'Why could we not cast him out?'

"So Jesus said to them, 'Because of your unbelief, for assuredly, I say to you, if you have faith as a mustard seed, you will say to this mountain, "Move from here to there," and it will move; and nothing will be impossible for you."'"

I want to burn the last part into your heart so that you will never forget it: *"And nothing will be impossible...."* If I stopped right there, it would be easy to agree with me. But if you read the entire clause, it says, *"And nothing will be impossible for **you**."*

Jesus meant it. That is why He gave us the privilege of stepping out in faith and laying hands on the sick, knowing they will be healed. As you just read, He said that nothing will be impossible for you. He didn't say for Me, because we all know that nothing is impossible for Him. To think that nothing is impossible for us, however, certainly changes our way of thinking.

The apostle Paul wrote, *"I can do all things through Christ who strengthens me" (Phil. 4:13).* We need to get that in our spirits and know we cannot do it on our own, but that we can do all things – whatever God calls us to do – through Christ who strengthens us.

Often when I lay hands on people, I pause before I start and say: *"I can do all things through Christ who strengthens me.*" Jesus made a positive statement in Mark 16: *"Those who believe; In My name they will lay hands on the sick, and they will recover" (vv. 17-18).* No ifs, ands or buts about it – *"those who believe will lay hands on the sick, and they will recover."*

John 14:12, one of my favorite verses, says, *"Most assuredly, I say to you, he who believes in Me, the works that I do he will do also; and greater works than these he will do, because I go to My Father."*

I didn't say that – Jesus did! As a believer, I have the right, the privilege and the authority to do even greater things than He did. Not only that, I have a responsibility to fulfill the Word of God in me because God lives in me, and Jesus lives in and through me. We need to believe that God's Word is speaking directly and personally to us in this twentieth century.

Every time a new year rolls around, both Charles and I get excited because we anticipate all the great and wonderful things God is going to do through us. Then when we reach the middle of the year, we look back and say: "God, we're so grateful for what You did in the first six months. Now what are You going to do in the last six months?" He always tops what He did the first six months!

We all need to be reminded of our potential, because we often forget that we can do all things through Christ who strengthens us. I can do greater things than Jesus did, not because I say it, but because He says it in His Word!

When you have confidence in God in you, then you will realize you don't have to answer every voice of criticism. When you get in the healing ministry, people will criticize you. But we need to understand that taking criticism is a part of anyone's life who is on the front lines. So instead of confidence in the critical things that someone may have said to you, you need to have confidence in God in you.

Step 4: Be Persistent

If you want to be successful in healing, you must be persistent. You cannot let go the first time somebody comes up to you and says: "Who do you think you are to lay hands on the sick?"

That can either crush you or inspire you to pray, "Thank You, Father, that Your Word says I can lay hands on the sick, and they will recover."

The primary reason that some people fizzle out after a healing class or explosion is because they fail to persist. Maybe on your first healing trip or mission you came against a hard case. To God no case is harder than another; but to us some seem harder than others. So we may encounter two or three people whom we classify as impossible cases. We think, I had three people with severed spinal cords, and not one of them got healed!

Don't get discouraged! Be persistent! Keep going!

One of the most persistent men in the Bible was Elisha. He got a vision of what he wanted, and hung on – and he got exactly what he wanted (II Kings 2).

Charles and I have often failed to see people healed. We have ministered to cancer victims who have died. But we have also ministered to many who lived. We keep right on going regardless of what happens, constantly learning more about healing in Jesus' name than we knew ten or fifteen years ago – or even one year ago. We are two of the most persistent people on earth.

Many people are healed when they quote, *"By His stripes I am healed."* It's wonderful when that happens.

But there are times when someone leaves a healing service looking just as bad as when he or she arrived.

I often laugh at Charles. He will call to the stage someone who has a back problem. Sometimes he does what we normally do, and the person doesn't get healed right away. If something doesn't work, Charles tries another prayer or command. He is persistent, and I have almost never seen someone with a back problem fail to be healed.

You can give up easily and say, "Well, it isn't working." Yes, it is, because in the final analysis, it will!

If you want to be a successful Christian – one who is alive to the Holy Spirit all the time – you must be persistent in every area of your life: in reading the Bible; in winning people to Jesus; in talking about Jesus. All of these things are vital.

Be persistent! Don't give up! The devil is the one who comes in and says, "It's not going to work." If you've ever laid hands on someone, you've more than likely had a visit from the devil before you ever took your hands off! He'll tell you that your Christianity won't work. But the Bible tells us that we're victorious in all things and more than conquerors. I constantly say that everything I put my hand to prospers.

Because I belong to Christ Jesus I am blessed with every spiritual blessing. Therefore it pleases God for me to walk in divine health.

You too, need to be persistent in speaking the Word of God over yourself. Be persistent; don't give up. No matter how many times the devil comes against you, don't you ever give up. No matter how many times you think you have failed, hang in there. Be persistent.

Step 5: Know What You Are Doing

You can be ignorant but sincere, and God will honor that. "My people perish for lack of knowledge." It will help tremendously, however, if you learn everything you can about healing. I often am amazed at some of the things I did when I first got saved.

For instance, at the first church in which I ever spoke, I gave an altar call and didn't know what to do when people responded. I don't think I believed anyone would answer the altar call, so when the first person came, I thought to myself, What am I going to do with the people who come up?

When others came and began to tell me their requests, I was dumbfounded. Finally I said, "As soon as I get home, I'll start praying." Isn't it wonderful that God will bless us in spite of our ignorance? But I discovered that if I was going to speak in churches, I needed to learn how to minister to people at the altar, to meet their needs right there and to introduce them to Jesus – the One who can give them the answer to every problem they might have.

Likewise, learn as much as you possibly can about healing. You can't learn too much. Charles and I are constantly learning new things about healing. The other night we were watching some videotapes of old healing services. Many were from the crusades of men such as A. A. Allen and William Branham, who were well-known years ago for their tremendous healings on the "Voice of

Healing" program. We watched a couple of hours of the actual live services they conducted, and we learned tremendous things from these men. Whenever we watch a healing service on television or go to someone else's healing service, we watch carefully to see if we can learn something new.

We love to watch the new "babies" at Healing Explosions. Sometimes they do things they never learned but apparently were instructed to do by the Holy Spirit. We see them doing things we never thought about doing or saying, and we discover that what they do is effective.

Learn everything you can about healing from successful people. Don't learn things from individuals who never have any successes in their healing attempts. Receive instruction from those who have had successful experiences and who know what they're doing!

Although Charles and I wrote the book "How to Heal the Sick," we still read it over and over because we forget some of the things we wrote. We watch the video tapes over and over, laughingly amazed at the fresh inspiration we receive from them each time. And every time I watch them, the Holy Spirit reminds me of something I have forgotten. When you watch those videos or read the book time and again, you'll learn something new every time.

Read the four Gospels and the book of Acts repeatedly to learn more about healing in the first-century church. I still read those five books more than any others because they talk about healing more than any other part of the Bible. If you want to learn how to heal, do the same things Jesus did. Say the same things Jesus said! You will be amazed at how effective that will be.

Two things bring miracles, and they go together – the name of Jesus and the power of God's Holy Spirit.

The power Jesus displayed in His miracles came from His Father. Jesus said, *"For the works which the Father has given Me to finish – the very works that I do – bear witness of Me ... that the Father has sent Me" (John 5:36).*

You also will be able to do miracles by using the name of Jesus and the power of God's Holy Spirit. Practice on everyone you can. Practice on your friends. Practice on your family and on yourself until you learn how to be proficient. The more you lay hands on the sick, the more proficient you'll become and the greater results you'll see.

Keep yourself prayed up! And keep yourself "read up" in the Bible at all times. Do what Jesus did!

Step 6: Talk About Your Successes, Not Your Failures

When Charles and I write or speak, we always talk about success. We never tell about the people who don't get healed – we tell about the ones who do. In doing this, we have discovered that the more we talk about success, the more people get healed. As we tell the victory stories, everyone's faith rises.

I recently heard about a lady brought to one of our Healing Explosions on a stretcher, dying of cancer. The doctors had allowed her to come because they said she had less than twenty-four hours to live. This was more than a year ago, and we just heard that she was completely healed by the power of God. Now she's telling everyone what Jesus did to her when she came to a Healing Explosion.

Those are the kinds of stories to tell – the success stories. One of my favorite Scripture verses is Philippians 4:8: *"Finally, brethren, whatever things are true, whatever things are noble, whatever things are just, whatever things are pure, whatever things are lovely, whatever things are of good report, if there is any virtue and if there is anything praiseworthy - meditate on these things."*

Think about the good things; think about the praiseworthy things. Think about that crippled person who got out of a wheelchair; think about that person with the horrible back problem who got healed when her legs grew out! Don't tell people about your failures – tell them about your successes!

Step 7: Get to Know Him

If you want to have success in ministering healing biblically, get to know Jesus in the power of His resurrection.

Psalm 27:1-4 in the Living Bible is tremendous. There is a real clue in here.

"The Lord is my light and my salvation; whom shall I fear? When evil men come to destroy me, they will stumble and fall! Yes, though a mighty army marches against me, my heart shall know no fear! I am confident that God will save me.

"The one thing I want from God, the thing I seek most of all, is the privilege of meditating in his Temple, living in his presence every day of my life, delighting in his incomparable perfections and glory."

I don't know what part of that verse spoke to you

the most clearly. But one day during a prayer meeting in our office, we asked the staff which part of that passage ministered to them the most.

One man said, "I'm most grateful for my salvation."

Another one said, "I just praise the Lord that He will protect me. Although an army marches against me, I will be protected."

Charles and I were thrilled the most by the part that says, *"The thing I seek the most of all is the privilege of meditating in his Temple, living in his presence every day of my life."*

When you get to know Jesus, you will have the same desires He has. The more you get to know Him, the closer you get to Him. The more intimate you become with Him, the more you will become like Him. The more you will have compassion in your heart to reach out to people who are lost, dying and sick.

The entire world desperately needs to know a living Jesus, but they also need you and me to introduce them to the One who is the answer to all of life's problems.

What an awesome privilege, yet what an equally awesome responsibility is given to us to bring the world to a living knowledge of the Lord Jesus Christ!

But what things were gain to me, these I have counted loss for Christ. Yet indeed I also count all things loss for the excellence of the knowledge of Christ Jesus my Lord, for whom I have suffered the loss of all things, and count them as rubbish, that I may gain Christ and be found in Him, not having my own righteousness, which is from the law, but that which is through faith in Christ, the righteousness which is from God by faith; that I may know Him and the power of His resurrection (Phil. 3:7-10).

Verses 12 through 14 expound on other great things: *Not that I have already attained, or am already perfected; but I press on, that I may lay hold of that for which Christ Jesus has also laid hold of me. Brethren, I do not count myself to have apprehended; but one thing I do, forgetting those things which are behind and reaching forward to those things which are ahead, I press toward the goal for the prize of the upward call of God in Christ Jesus."*

"I press toward the goal." Probably Paul's greatest desire was to know Him. To know Him more intimately than I can even dream possible is the desire of my heart.

The day I got saved I heard a song that said,

> "Turn your eyes upon Jesus,
> look full in His wonderful face.
> And the things of earth will
> grow strangely dim in the
> light of His glory and grace."*

The more you get to know Him, the dimmer the things of this earth will become and the less hold they will have on you. Put all of these seven steps into practice; think about them and meditate upon them. I guarantee they will lead you to success in ministering healing biblically.

Keep it up, remembering you are doing your part to usher in the King of Kings and the Lord of lords.

And you are...

well-equipped and dangerously loaded
and have the ability to explode all over!

(Frances)

Chapter Twenty-Two

Michelle – High School Student

Things were pretty easy as long as Michelle wasn't attending public school. For some time her mother had home-schooled her. But now it had become necessary for her to start back to public school. Her mind was flooded with questions. Could she maintain her Christian witness? Could she even maintain her Christian attitude? She was about to find out!

Several weeks had gone by and things seemed to be working okay. She had made some new friends, met a lot of new people, and generally was holding her own.

Then it happened! In the school gym! Right in the middle of a volleyball game! The ball was hit with all the power the hitter could muster. Like a white cannonball it zipped through several hands, and hit Jason full force, right in the side of his head! The force knocked him up against the wall, his head making contact with the wall first.

Michelle had seen the whole thing. And now, she saw Jason sitting on the floor holding his head, plainly in pain.

He spoke very clearly, this voice deep down inside her. A voice she had heard before, even at her young age. This voice, the silent voice of the Holy Spirit, instructed her to go immediately and pray for Jason and he would be healed.

"But Lord, I can't do that!" she responded in her mind.

To that, this still small voice of assurance replied, "That's right! But you're not doing the work, I am!"

With that answer, Michelle approached Jason and asked him if it would be all right if she asked Jesus to heal him.

"Yes..... *Please!* It can't hurt any more than it's hurting now!" was Jason's reply.

Michelle gently laid her hands on his head and commanded, "In the name *of Jesus* I command *this swelling to go* down and the pain *to stop!"* With her co-students watching in awe, all the swelling and the pain went away, right then, at once!

Someone else had been watching! Someone not really knowing what was going on! The gym teacher did not like what she saw, nor what she was told had happened. The anger was evident. It was in her eyes and in her voice. "You have no right to do that sort of thing here," she lashed out at Michelle! "You're expressing your 'faith' at school, and besides, we have a school nurse to take care of that type of thing!"

Michelle disagreed! "All I did was pray for him to stop hurting!"

"You have no right to pray at school," the teacher retorted!

But even as they "exchanged views", the Holy Spirit had placed an ambush. The volleyball game was still going on. Suddenly a cry of pain, and the sight of all the players rushing to a fallen form on the floor! The girl had jumped and lost her balance as she came down. Her knee had struck the floor first and her knee had been knocked out of joint. The damage could be seen by anyone looking on because the dislocated knee joint could be plainly seen under the skin.

With an air of arrogance, the gym teacher turned to Michelle. "OK! See if your God is really powerful. Pray for her!"

The first thought to invade Michelle's mind was doubt, then a question, "Oh no! This is all I need! Why?" But again that impression from down deep, "Go!" So she did! She laid her hands on the injured knee. The girl winced in pain. Michelle spoke to the knee! "In Jesus' name I command healing to this knee." Nothing! Sweat began to bead on Michelle's forehead.

"Please, Lord!" she cried in her heart. "You didn't bring me to this point for nothing!"

Then with a flash of inspiration she asked Shelly, "Do you believe God can heal you?" Through the tears came a muffled, "Yes!"

Now, in Michelle's spirit, she senses the release.

Now with authority she spoke to the knee: "In the name *of Jesus I* command this knee and all *the bones* within that knee to line up, in Jesus' name!"

The students are watching - waiting!

The gym teacher is watching - waiting!

And there, before their startled eyes, the bones began to move back into place. Among the watchers, some gasps! Someone says, "Jesus"...but this time not as a swear **word,** but in awe!

Suddenly Shelly begins to scream, "Thank you *Jesus!* Thank you *Jesus!*

In shock and conditioned unbelief, the gym teacher just stares.

Now things are certainly different for Michelle at public school. Still not sure of what she saw, or just what happened that day, the gym teacher knows what to do when a student is injured in gym class.

Besides, with Michelle and the Lord, all that paper work is eliminated!

If Michelle can do it, you can do it, too!

Chapter Twenty-Three

As You Are Going...

When Jesus told us to go, He meant "as you are going"– going about your daily business, at work, in school, at the park, at the shopping center, before and after church, in the restaurant, at the health club, at prayer meetings, at coffee or lunch breaks or wherever your daily life takes you. We should be fulfilling the Great Commission on a continual daily basis.

Walk, run or fly with us through a few of the lifestyle events of our normal daily walk with Jesus!

Flying to a meeting one day, the man sitting next to us stood up. We noticed a special back pillow in his seat.

To us that was a signal for a miracle. When he returned, we questioned him about his back.

He was a salesman who traveled overseas as well as in the United States. He said the pain was so excruciating that he didn't believe he would be able to make it to Korea the next week.

As we were getting off the plane in the next city, we asked him, "Would you like to go to the lobby and let us pray for your back to be healed?" When you're hurting badly enough, you will never resist such an offer. We told him he had nothing to lose.

He was in such severe pain as he hobbled to the lobby that he was almost in tears. He didn't want to sit down in public, so we put him behind the ticket counter wall.

His back was so out of line, we discovered, that one leg was two inches shorter than the other. When it grew out, he jumped up, bent over, twisted his back and then heard, "Final boarding call!" He ran down the ramp as fast as he could, yelling, "I have no more pain!"

Another healing occurred on a recent trip when we stopped at "the only open at that hour of the night" restaurant on this trip. After seating us at a dirty, oil-cloth-covered table, the waitress gave us the menus. Charles noticed something. He said to the waitress: "My wife has a wonderful ministry for pregnant women. Would you like for her to pray for you?"

The young woman burst into laughter and said, "Pray?" and continued laughing.

I immediately sensed a wonderful "as we were going" opportunity. So, grabbing her left hand, I laid my hand on her tummy and said, "Father, I thank You for this beautiful baby. Thank You that we don't believe in abortion." Before I said another word, she burst into tears. I knew she had considered abortion. I asked her whether she was married because there was no ring on her finger. She stumbled for words and finally came out with a very weak, "Yes."

I said, "You need Jesus, honey. Pray this prayer after me."

She prayed, and when we finished, I asked her, "Where is Jesus right now?"

She said, "In my heart!" The girl we left behind was not the same girl we met when we came in. She was a new creature!

You will notice that we have mentioned the fifteen hour video healing tapes on *HOW TO HEAL THE SICK*. This is one of the most invaluable tools that God has ever given to the body of Christ to teach them how to minister healing successfully. These same tapes have also been translated into languages so that 80% of the world's population can listen to them in their own native language and read the book, *HOW TO HEAL THE SICK*, in their own native language.

For further information about the *HOW TO HEAL THE SICK* video tapes and the books by Charles and Frances Hunter, *HOW TO HEAL THE SICK*, *HANDBOOK FOR HEALING*, and *THE SUPERNATURAL SPINE*, as well as others, call (281) 358-7575 or contact Hunter Books via e-mail at wec@cfhunter.org.

The video tapes and the three books mentioned above will also be invaluable in teaching you, "If Charles and Frances can do it, <u>YOU CAN DO IT, TOO!</u>" Many of the things we have discussed lightly in this book are covered in more detail in the other healing books.